STARTING
OVER AGAIN

STARTING OVER AGAIN

JOANNE WALLACE

AND

DEANNA WALLACE

THOMAS NELSON PUBLISHERS
Nashville

Published in Nashville, Tennessee, by Thomas Nelson,
Inc., Publishers, and distributed in Canada by Word
Communications, Ltd., Richmond, British Columbia,
and in the United Kingdom by Word (UK), Ltd., Milton
Keynes, England.

Unless otherwise noted, Scripture quotations are from
THE NEW KING JAMES VERSION. Copyright © 1979,
1980, 1982, Thomas Nelson, Inc., Publishers.

Scripture marked NAVIGATORS is from the Navigators
Paraphrased Version.

Library of Congress Cataloging-in-Publication Data

Wallace, Joanne.
    Starting over again / Joanne Wallace and Deanna
Wallace.
        p.   cm.
    Includes bibliographical references.
    ISBN 0-8407-3048-9 (pbk.)
    1. Consolation.   2. Loss (Psychology)—Religious
aspects—Christianity.   3. Adjustment
(Psychology)—Religious aspects—Christianity.
    4. Life change events—Psychological aspects.
    5. Christian life—1960–   I. Wallace, Deanna.
    II. Title.
BV4905.2.W35   1991
248.8'6—dc20   90–23569
                                                CIP

Printed in the United States of America
5 6 7 8 9 10 — 99 98 97

Dedication

To our family—
our loves—
who make it possible
to start over again:
Bob Lovelace and Robby,
Aron, Kimmi, Jameson,
Shaina, and Fallon Early.

Other Books by Joanne Wallace:

The Image of Loveliness
Dress With Style
The Confident Woman
The Working Woman
Dress to Fit Your Personality
How to be Your Best

Contents

Acknowledgments

*To Pastor Claude Robold,
for your invaluable wisdom and insights.*

*To Pastor Tom Wilson,
for your support, love, and encouragement.*

*To Donna Hartley,
for your friendship, knowledge, honesty, and love.*

*To the women who have shared
their lives and experiences so that others might be
helped by this book. Throughout this book I have
changed names and disguised circumstances to preserve
their privacy.*

PROOF:
You Can Always Start Over Again

Hang in there! Don't give up!
Don't give up on your optimism or your vision.
George Washington never gave up.
Abraham Lincoln never gave up.
Oliver Twiddledee . . . who's he?
See, you don't know him—
BECAUSE HE GAVE UP!

—Lacie Abel

CHAPTER ONE

I had just waved good-bye to the women who had attended a Bible study in my home that evening in the spring of 1986. It had been a good time of learning and sharing, but the burdens on my heart made me feel out of touch. The material we'd studied was on "crisis management"—a subject in which I desperately needed help as I felt devastated by my own crisis.

As I walked down the hall to the office in my home I reviewed the information we'd covered. Although the material was good for many situations in life, somehow I just couldn't identify with it. The answer that was given for life's crises was summed up in, "Just turn it over to Jesus and relax." With the deep inner turmoil I was feeling, I had wanted to cry out to the women at the Bible study, "You don't understand! Sometimes the pain is so deep and the situations so complex that an easy answer cannot cover it."

Sitting down at my office desk, the pain began to wash over me in waves. I sat with my face in my hands, my body bowed over my desk as I sobbed and sobbed. My world was shattered. Crisis after crisis had developed in my life until each had finally exploded. I felt utterly destroyed, brought to the point of wishing for death. Even if I'd been able to completely "turn it over to Jesus," there was no way I would have been able to relax.

As I sat at my desk weeping, I remembered what my life had been like just three years before, in early 1983. I was in my forties and felt that my life had been a success in all areas. My two children were grown and responsible adults. My son, Bob, was a college graduate with a great business future who had moved to Europe to further his career. My daughter, Deanna, was married to a chiropractor, and they were busy raising my darling grandchildren. My husband and I were running our corporation and I thought we were seeing much growth.

In 1969, I had compiled and started teaching a self-improvement course for women called "The Image of Loveliness." This eight-week course became very popular and eventually I formed Image Improvement, Inc., in order to train teachers for Image courses worldwide.

My personal speaking career was also on the rise. At that time I was booked for church-sponsored seminars more than one year in advance, had authored four books, and had my own nationally syndicated Christian television program.

My personal and financial future looked great. My husband and I had just moved into a big, beautiful home on top of a hill in Salem, Oregon. Our children and grandchildren were happy. I was confident that my marriage was secure and I would never become a divorce statistic.

I had often boasted of my wonderful, unshakeable marriage from the speaker's platform. In fact, when I look back at that time, I realize that I was living in a fairy tale, and unfortunately, real life does not always provide a happy ending.

How quickly a life can shatter! Like a stick of dynamite with a long fuse, the fuse of my problems was burning for years, but I didn't realize it. When the explosions came, culminating in a period of just thirty days, I was totally overwhelmed.

The first and most devastating explosion came with the

final signing of divorce papers to dissolve my twenty-eight-year marriage. This was the most painful, tragic, and unbelievable experience of my life. The grief was so great, at times I didn't think I could survive.

My marriage had been slowly disintegrating, but unintentionally, I ignored the danger signs. In 1983 I sensed that there was something seriously wrong, but my husband denied it, and I wanted desperately to believe him, so I let time drift by without insisting on steps for improvement. With great sadness, I can now see that we pursued our careers and other interests while not taking the time to nurture our relationship.

The following year I asked my husband to go to marriage enrichment weekends or counseling with me, but something in our busy schedules always prevented it. That same year, I also had a hysterectomy. Since my husband still claimed nothing was wrong in our relationship, I tried to convince myself that the problems were due to the emotional trauma and fluctuating hormone levels. Once again, I let time drift by without any improvement in our relationship.

By 1985 my marriage was in desperate trouble. I could no longer deny it. My marriage finally disintegrated when certain events destroyed the deep trust my husband and I had shared. Neither counseling nor a trial separation was able to help. To my disbelief and great sorrow, divorce became a reality in my life.

I believe God's plan for marriage means "till death do you part." Anything less is not God's perfect plan. Sometimes, however, no matter how much I wish it were otherwise, God's perfect plan is destroyed by man's sin. Tragically, this is what happened in my life.

I know what it's like to rebuild from ashes. I've endured what I thought seemed impossible to endure. The divorce was the most horrible, crushing, and appalling experience of my life. There were days when I literally felt I couldn't get out of bed, as though I were physically falling into a dark tunnel, as a deep, sinking pressure enveloped me. At times I would be overtaken with nausea, but more often with uncontrollable sobbing.

During my crisis experience, the irreparable breakup of my marriage was by far the worst explosion, but it wasn't the only one. While I was in that thirty-day crisis period I also experienced three other explosions, spreading rampant destruction in my life.

One of the explosions came with the news that my corporation was being hit with a major lawsuit. My wonderful secretary delayed informing me so that I could enjoy a "good weekend." As it turned out, however, the newspapers got hold of the story and printed it in the Saturday papers. That's how I found out about it!

Not one of my insurance policies would cover the cost of the lawsuit, which was filed for over $150,000. Along with the potential financial drain, there was also the very real expense of hiring attorneys to fight the case in court. Because of the time and energy needed to cope with the situation, and also the psychological stress for myself, my staff, and my Image teachers, the financial and emotional tolls that this lawsuit represented were enormous.

Another explosion came when an IRS audit loomed on the horizon. Unfortunately, my company's business consultants had given misleading information about tax-deductible items; therefore, the audit revealed that unexpected amounts of money were owed to the government. These amounts, with interest, were close to $50,000.

My marriage had disintegrated, and my financial and business life was facing ruin. I felt that my only hope for survival lay in my still-prospering speaking career. So with this hope burning inside me, I planned to travel to Tacoma, Washington, where I was to be the featured speaker and seminar leader for several hundred women at a local church.

The day before my speaking engagement, I traveled to my parents' home with my daughter, Deanna, and my grandchildren to combine a family visit with my business trip. That night I awoke to a chilly room. Concerned that my grandson, Aron, might be uncovered, I went to check on him. A small step separated our rooms. Assuring myself that he was sufficiently warm, I returned to my room. But in my sleepy state I forgot about the step, tripped, and fell in excruciating pain. I had landed exactly the wrong way on my ankle and had to be taken to the emergency room.

Instead of speaking before several hundred women the next day, I was flat on my back with a cast on my leg, enduring some of the worst physical pain I'd ever felt. Not only did I have to cancel the speaking engagement in Tacoma, but all of my upcoming engagements for the next two months! My last hope had exploded like the rest of my life.

How could so many life-changing things happen to me in a period of thirty days? How could I ever go on? I felt worthless, a washout, a has-been. It didn't matter that many of the problems were out of my control. I spent hours in remorse, going over all my "if onlys." I wanted so desperately to undo the past, but of course, that was impossible.

There is nothing worse than hopelessness. Without hope, life loses its meaning. Without hope, every day, every minute is unendurable. At the point of hopelessness people commit suicide, and at times I, too, longed for death. Some days the pain was so great I could hardly think. My mind had stagnated on simple questions. What do I do today? Is there anyone who understands? At times I felt I couldn't even pray, I hurt so much.

So there I was, that evening in the spring of 1986, sitting at my desk, weeping uncontrollably, reliving each crisis, and feeling hopeless. How could I "turn it over to Jesus and relax"?

Finally, sitting there with my face in my hands, I knew I had to do something to rouse myself out of the pain. Although I'd already spent counseling time with my pastor, there was an urgent need to make another appointment the next day.

I'll never forget that meeting with my pastor, Tom Wilson. At first I couldn't even find the words to speak. I sat there sobbing, just as I had the night before at my desk. I was sure that my usefulness on earth had ended. The next logical step was to find a cabin out in the woods somewhere and live out the rest of my life in seclusion. So strong was this thought that when I was finally able to speak, I asked my pastor if he knew where I could find such a place! In all my despair I looked at him and said, "Don't you think it's time for me to retire?"

With great kindness, gentleness, and firmness this dear man of God looked right back at me and said, "Joanne, are you going to quit? Don't you know that's exactly what Satan wants you to do? If he can get you to quit, he's won."

In my confused and hopeless state, this simple truth had never crossed my mind. I stared at him as this new truth settled into my consciousness. Pastor Tom then went on to say, "Joanne, dream a new dream. Pray for a new dream. You just can't quit."

As he said those words God began a new work within me. It was still a very small seed, and I still needed much healing, but after claiming God's promises through a time of prayer in my pastor's office, I left with the truth implanted in my mind: No matter what, never give up, because you can always start over again.

Several years have passed since the explosions that shattered my life caused me to sit weeping at my desk. Since that time I've learned that God's great mercy, love, and grace through Jesus Christ can rebuild broken lives and dreams. No matter what has happened to you, it does not have to be the end of life. God promises to rebuild your life too. I have been able to pick up the pieces of my shattered life and start again. You'll see how in the coming chapters, and you'll recognize some steps that you can take as you start over again too.

I am now over the age of fifty. For those of you who are younger, fifty is traditionally the post-menopausal period in a woman's life when she is supposed to feel *old*. Not exactly a fun idea, but one that many women believe. I'm embarrassed to admit that when I first turned fifty, I, too, felt *old*. Once again I had the idea that maybe my usefulness on this earth was about over!

Around this time a friend, Dr. Harold Ivan Smith, came to town to give a seminar. I contacted him and we made arrangements to chat during the afternoon break.

Over a cup of tea in a local restaurant, Harold heard me say, "I'm over the hill, Harold. I've just had my fiftieth birthday." I felt it would be impossible to start over in some areas, now that I was "too old."

He looked at me with wide eyes and said, "Joanne, what do you mean, 'too old'? Don't you know how many people became successful and contributed to society *after* they turned fifty? What about Grandma Moses? Mother Teresa?"

I sat there listening to him and began to feel rather sheepish. Once again, someone was turning on the bright light of truth in my brain. Finally I found the courage to quietly mutter, "I guess you're right. You can always start over again."

After Harold's pep talk I began once again to see possibilities. As Sophia Loren, at age fifty-five, said, "You shouldn't drag yourself down because you turn fifty. If you have achieved something in life, age doesn't scare you."

As you contemplate starting over again, it may seem an impossible task. Unless you have been there it is difficult to adequately explain the disturbing adjustment, the deep remorse, loneliness, and fears preceding or following a major life change. It doesn't matter what caused the change—separation, divorce, death, career change, or any other source. What matters is realizing and dealing with the damage and distortions those changes can bring—damage to self, family, friends, career, and other personal relationships.

Putting together the shattered pieces of your life is a day and night, full-time job that demands enormous energy. When there has been extreme pain and hurt, it may take extreme time to heal. *Take the time.* There are too many people who think that everything has to have a quick cure. You may hear "just turn it over to Jesus and relax." But I've found that starting over is a healing *process* with a series of steps you must go through. This book will help take you through the process. The important thing right now is that you begin to *believe* that starting over is possible.

A while ago I gave a seminar at the First Presbyterian Church in Coral Ridge, Florida, whose senior pastor is Dr. D. James Kennedy. After a full day of speaking I had the privilege of having dinner with Dr. and Mrs. Kennedy. Considering the way God has blessed Dr. Kennedy's ministry, I asked him, "What one word would express your feelings as you see all the grand and marvelous ways God has used you?" With softness, gentleness, and a humbleness that is not often seen in such a well-known personality he said, "Gratitude."

As I recall Dr. Kennedy's answer my heart, too, is full of gratitude. I'm so grateful for God's love and for the opportunity that He provides to start over. I'm grateful, and also humbled, because even though my life was once shattered, God did not abandon me; He still chooses to work in and through me.

I want to assure you that God will not abandon you either. Your personal pain, sorrow, and heartache matter to Him. Regardless of what has happened in your life, God wants to help, assist, and strengthen you, so that you can begin anew.

The choice is yours. You can stay where you are, or you can decide to pick up the pieces and start over again. Making the choice to start over again is the first step toward the promising future God has in store for you. As an old Chinese proverb says, "The journey of a thousand miles begins with one step." I hope that you'll take that first step and decide to start over again, today.

GRIEF:
The Necessary Healing Process

If we respond to adversities with cynicism
and unresolved anger,
we become hardened in spirit.
If we keep trusting God and obeying Him,
His wonderful comfort
makes us grow tender.

—Unknown

CHAPTER TWO

My grandson, Robby, was born in Calcutta, India, and lived the first several years of his life with his birth parents. One day the whole city was preparing for an annual Hindu celebration. Statues of the Hindu gods were being paraded through the town and the streets were swarming with cars and people. Everyone was out having a good time, watching fireworks and celebrating. On that day Robby, then about six years old, was out on the streets with everyone else when his uncle drove past in a truck carrying one of the statues of the gods. Adults and children were climbing on the backs of the flatbed trucks as they drove slowly through the crowds, and Robby decided to join them. Feeling very independent and without consulting his parents, he scrambled onto the back of the truck. Surrounded by many other celebrants, all laughing and smiling, he thought this was one of the best days of his life. He felt sure that the truck would eventually bring him back by his house since his uncle was driving, so he wasn't worried.

Unfortunately, Robby hadn't counted on the size of the crowd, nor their jubilation and excitement. Many more people tried to climb on the truck as the parade made its way through the streets of Calcutta. At some point, quite a distance from Robby's home in an area he had never seen before, an excited celebrant accidentally pushed him off the end of the truck and into the teeming crowd. According to Robby's account, no one even noticed him fall; the truck never slowed down.

Suddenly thrown into an unfamiliar mass of people, Robby had no idea where he was or how to get home. Alone, frightened, and lost, he began crying for his parents. Someone on the street gave him a little money, and as night fell he had no choice but to curl up on the sidewalk and try to get some sleep.

In the morning Robby's money was gone, stolen while he slept. Again he cried and finally attracted the attention of a passerby who took pity on him and told Robby he would help him get back to his parents. Robby went with the man to his home where he called the police.

When the police arrived, they took Robby to a place where hundreds of other lost children are taken every year in India—to a government run "home," which Robby refers to as "jail." Robby never saw his birth parents again. *In one night he lost his whole identity*—his parents, brothers and sisters, his home, and any sense of security. Everything familiar to him was taken away in an instant. I cannot even imagine such an all-encompassing loss happening to me!

For the next several years Robby lived in the children's "jails" in Calcutta. During that time he had plenty of opportunity to grieve for his family. For the longest time he waited and hoped that his parents would find him, but it never happened. Calcutta is a large city, over 12 million people, in a small area. Many people cannot read the newspapers. India has over 1,000 different languages and dialects. Since Robby's parents were very poor and most probably illiterate, they did not know how to find him. In fact, the most common reason older children are available for adoption from India is that they are separated from their families. Robby's story is not even an unusual one.

Robby learned to survive on his own, but he never gave

up the dream of being reunited with his family. Finally, after years of disappointment he was told that he was going to be adopted by a family in the United States. Although he didn't fully understand what this meant—in fact he now says he thought he was returning to his birth parents—he was very excited.

Three years ago at age ten, Robby arrived in America to join our family. My daughter, Deanna, and her husband, Dean, became his new parents. Robby's life changed materially and emotionally for the better. He now has an opportunity to get an education, is well-clothed and fed, and most importantly, is nurtured and loved. You'd think he would feel only joy, but you're wrong. Robby still feels sad sometimes and cries about the loss of his birth parents. He still thinks about them and wonders what has happened to them. Although Robby loves his new family very much and says that he is so happy to be with them, he also realizes an important aspect of grief—*no one is ever replaced.*

Before you can truly start over in life, you may find that you need to grieve for the loss you have experienced. Whatever the cause of your loss—death, divorce, job loss, victimization, or betrayal—it is important that you allow yourself the opportunity to grieve.

Regardless of whether your marriage was a living hell and you are glad to be out of the situation, the fact is that you experienced a major loss when you were divorced and, good or bad, that loss brings grief that needs to be released. This is true for every experience of loss in life.

You may start over in life, you may get to the point where you realize your life is better now than it used to be, you may even be experiencing real love and security, but it is important to remember this: No one and no thing is ever replaced in your life. Since this is true, the grieving process *must* be experienced whenever there is a loss in our lives.

If you have experienced or are experiencing a loss in your life, the following list may help you understand normal behavior experienced by children and adults during the grieving process.

1. You have an empty feeling in your stomach; you may not feel like eating.
2. You feel as if the loss didn't really happen. You think you'll wake up one day and it will have been a dream.
3. You expect the lost person to return at any moment.
4. You are reminded often, by smells, sounds, and places, of the person you lost.
5. You feel restless but at the same time have trouble concentrating.
6. You wander and feel confused, sometimes forgetting what you are doing and forgetting to finish what you have started.
7. You have frequent dreams about the lost person and may have a hard time sleeping.
8. You try to become the lost person and finish things he or she didn't get done.
9. You feel guilty or angry over things that happened in the past with the lost person.
10. Your mood changes often and you cry at unexpected times.

All of these feelings are normal when you lose something that is important to you. Remember that it is necessary to *cry* and to *talk* to other people when you feel the need. Dealing with your grief and letting your feelings out will make it easier for you to get on with your new life.

Elisabeth Kübler-Ross, psychiatrist and authority on death, has identified five different stages of grief. When you have experienced a loss, no matter how big or small, you will undoubtedly experience these five stages:

1. Shock and Denial
2. Anger

3. Bargaining
4. Depression
5. Acceptance/Adjustment

I'll illustrate these stages through a minor experience in my own life, which demonstrates how even when the loss is small, the stages stay the same.

Not too long ago I lost my car keys. At first I just couldn't believe it and searched all over the house for them. I was in the first stage: *shock* and *denial*.

A few minutes later I was *angry*. I was angry at myself for losing the keys and also angry because I was tired of searching for them. I was mad because I had no control over the situation.

When I started thinking a little more rationally I went into the *bargaining* stage. At this point I thought if I just calmed down and tried to remember where the keys were it might help. I even prayed and asked God to help me find the keys. If I could just find the keys I promised I'd take better care of them.

When I still didn't find the keys I became *depressed*. It dawned on me that I was going to be stuck in the house all day. What a mess! I might as well just give up. After all, I'd looked everywhere and couldn't find them. The situation was hopeless, right?

Of course, it didn't take long to rouse myself out of depression and realize that I had no choice but to *accept* the situation and make the most of it. I had to *adjust* my schedule around my lack of keys. It turned out that it wasn't such a bad day after all, and I got a lot accomplished around the house. I did eventually find my keys wedged between the back of the sofa and the wall.

In this instance, the stages of grief were accomplished in a very short period of time, which is not uncommon when the loss is small. However, when your loss is a major one, the grief process can take months and years to accomplish

In fact, some people can even get stuck in one of the stages.

Getting stuck in a grief stage can have some very serious repercussions. Unresolved grief keeps you in bondage to the pain and devastation caused by your loss. How can you work through your grief and into a new life? A close examination of the grieving process should give you some insight, although you may not experience the stages in exactly this order or you may skip around between stages.

Shock and Denial

Getting stuck in the shock and denial stage usually happens because the loss was very unexpected and took you totally by surprise. Lisa, a precious friend of mine, was a victim of rape at the age of sixteen. Her loss was one of innocence. Frightened, guilt-ridden, and ashamed, she felt unable to tell her parents what had happened. In her mind and upbringing "bad things didn't happen to good Christians." Her pain and isolation were compounded by the mistaken idea that if her parents knew of the rape, they would accuse and blame her. At that point in her life the shock and sense of disbelief were overwhelming. Her mind kept reiterating, *This isn't happening to me. This is not real.* After the rape she kept her secret and stuffed the memory away. Lisa stayed in denial for fourteen years.

During those fourteen years she made many wrong choices. Subconsciously she felt that control of her life had been taken away by the rapist. She wanted to regain that control and wrongly chose promiscuous sexual behavior as the path. Subliminally she told herself, *If I no longer have my virginity, at least I can choose my own sexual partner. I'm going to use my sexuality to my advantage to gain back power in my life.* Step by step, wrong choice compounded by wrong choice, she added misery and pain to her life.

Staying in the denial stage is very sad because you stay

in bondage to the past hurt and loss and are never able to release the pain and begin to start anew.

Continuing in the denial stage also damages your self-image. By not talking about the loss you have experienced, you leave yourself open to unjustifiable self-recrimination. For fourteen years Lisa told herself the lie that somehow she was to blame for the rape, that she was an unclean person, therefore worthless. Her sexual involvement with other men confirmed what she'd been telling herself—she was not a valuable person. Although she did eventually give up promiscuity, get married, and have children, the problems didn't go away. She still felt a tremendous need for control.

What eventually happened in Lisa's life is what usually happens to anyone who gets stuck in denial. The feelings and emotions she had left so long buried finally broke through to the surface. Lisa began having flashbacks in which she relived the panic, pain, and rage she had felt at the time of the rape. Any situation where she felt out of control would trigger a flashback. Eventually she became enraged even when her children were slightly disobedient, and she felt she couldn't cope.

Making the decision to seek help was very difficult, but she finally consulted with a good Christian therapist and was able to admit aloud what had happened to her so many years before. This opened the door on her imprisoned pain and helped begin the long, slow process of healing in her life.

Many times, hurts from our childhood are suppressed in adulthood. Coming through the denial stage means you can admit that the hurt occurred and you are ready to start dealing with it. You have a very simple choice to make: are you going to allow the wrong that has been done to you to continue to devastate your life?

Depending on your situation, you may say, "I was abused. I was violated as a child and it hurt me physically and emotionally. I didn't deserve what happened to me and I have suppressed the memory. It has guided some of my decisions and caused some of my decisions to perhaps be wrong, but at this point I am ready to deal with it." If you can say this, the next statement you need to say and believe is this: My past hurts are not going to be the guiding force in my life any longer.

The enemy against your soul, Satan, wants you to keep the hurt locked within you. He wants to keep you in bondage, but the Lord wants to deliver you. Satan tells you, "You are at fault. You deserve this. You're a worthless person." Satan uses this spirit of accusation to keep you from being free of the hurt.

If you're stuck in the denial stage and feel that you just can't admit to yourself or to anyone else what has happened in your life, I urge you right now to take one positive step. In the privacy of your own home, when you are all alone, speak to yourself in an audible voice and tell yourself the loss you have experienced. If you can hear yourself say it out loud, it will be easier to deal with your pain. If you can come to the point where you can actually tell another person about the painful loss you've experienced, you'll be well on your way to dealing with your grief. I hope and pray that if you are still in denial about your pain that your bondage will end today.

I can remember so well a similar step I had to take in my own life. For many months I was in a state of denial about the fact that I was getting divorced. No one outside close friends and family were aware of the divorce. I couldn't believe that it was actually happening to me. During a counseling session, my pastor, Tom Wilson, said to me, "Joanne, you've really got to face this issue in your life. I'd like you to come join the divorce recovery workshop group that meets here at the church on Tuesday nights." His request caught me completely off-guard, and I found myself agreeing to come the following Tuesday night.

Before I knew it Tuesday night arrived and I drove to the church and parked outside. That was as far as I could go. I couldn't get out of the car. I was starting to realize that by joining the group I was admitting to myself and to the world the fact that I was getting divorced. Reality came crashing in on my denial and I began to cry uncontrollably. The racking sobs seemed to be torn from my soul as I started to truly face what was happening in my life.

After many minutes my sobs gradually subsided and I decided to muster my courage and join the group inside the church.

As I looked around for a place to sit two women recognized me and immediately came over to greet me. One of them said, "Oh, I know why you're here. You're going to write a book about divorce and use us as research material!"

At that moment I almost walked out the door. I couldn't respond to this woman. Inside I was crying, *I'm not studying you, I'm ONE of you!*, but I just couldn't say it out loud yet.

I was rescued from this awkward moment when one of the leaders of the group, Pastor Steve Bearden, came over and said, "This is very difficult for you, isn't it Joanne?" Again I started to cry and he asked, "Do you need a hug?"

In that instant I had a choice to make. I could either be honest, say yes, and receive the hug I so desperately needed, or I could say no and wallow in the pain and resentment I was keeping inside. The difficulty was made worse in that a man was asking if I needed a hug! At that point in time men were definitely on my "I'd rather go to the dentist" list!

Hesitating for a moment, I finally said yes and got the hug I needed. That hug helped to give me confidence so that I could stay at the meeting. Although that first night I sat alone in the back of the room, I was there! It was the beginning of a whole new outlook for me. I learned that only when you face your situation in the cold light of reality can you ever hope to truly get on with your life.

Anger

Anger is one of the most common deadlocks in the grieving process. When we experience a loss we naturally feel angry, even outrage, at the injustice of our situation.

During my crisis experience, I felt ANGER—and the capital letters are not an exaggeration. I had boasted from the speaker's platform about my "solid" marriage. Many audiences had heard me say that I would be married forever—I believed in one man, one woman for life, and I still do. But to my sorrow, our world is far from perfect.

In my smugness I can remember being very judgmental when I heard that someone I knew was getting a divorce. I'd think, *Tsk. Tsk. Don't you know divorce is wrong? What's the matter with you?*

When divorce became a reality in my own life, I felt outraged and utterly humiliated. I found myself constantly asking, "How could this happen?" and when I couldn't get all the answers, it made me even angrier. Naturally I wanted to place blame—sometimes I blamed myself for not realizing my marital problems, and at other times I angrily blamed my former husband.

When my anger overwhelmed me I had to learn positive ways to vent it. If I'd kept it inside me, I would have gone crazy. I'm so grateful to the Nazarene women in the Bible study I was involved in at the time. Through some of our meetings I could do nothing but cry tears of hurt and anger. These Spirit-filled women never condemned me or told me to "snap out of it." Betty Jo Kinler, one of the leaders, gently said, "It's okay to feel angry. It's normal." What a gift she and the others gave to me—the priceless gift of acceptance, as they provided a way for me to express my pain and anger.

Remember this: your feelings will always come out, either through your actions or your words. The women in my Bible study allowed me to vent my feelings in a positive way. Not once did they pounce on me, reprimand, or silence me. They were "image bearers" of Jesus to me.

For true healing to come in your life you've got to talk about your anger, betrayal, rejection, or loneliness. Don't let it get the best of you and come out through destructive actions and revenge. Recently Ann Landers printed a letter in her column that dealt with this very issue. The letter said in part:

> The beatings I received from my mother for as far back as I can remember were brutal. . . . I started to run away from that hellish house when I was 5. I got ulcers at 12 and attempted suicide at 13. . . .
>
> Now comes the kicker, Ann. Mom had no financial problems and I was perfectly legitimate. It was my mother who was the unwanted child. . . .Grandma ate gunpowder trying to abort, but it didn't work. My mother was put in boarding school from the time she was 6 years old. I realize now that everything my mother did to me was done to her. All the rage and rejection that she felt made her want to get even, and I was the target.

As this letter indicates, unexpressed anger comes out in our actions, and usually we take it out on an innocent person.

My friend Lisa dealt with repressed anger all of her adult life. Struggling to be a "good Christian," she felt she never measured up. Because of the sexual abuse she suffered, her anger vented itself upon her husband and children. If her children accidentally spilled their milk at dinner, Lisa would come unglued. Any simple, childish accident would be enough to set off her rage. Although she couldn't stand the look of bewilderment and hurt in her children's eyes, she didn't know how else to cope.

Lisa's life began to change when she started to deal with the source, not the symptoms, of her anger. She can now defuse her anger through counseling and discussion. If you feel that unresolved anger is a chronic problem for you, there may be underlying reasons. Fred and Florence Littauer, in their excellent book, *Freeing Your Mind from Memories that Bind,* suggest that a problem with uncontrolled anger may have its roots in past childhood sexual abuse. There may be an incident or incidents in your past that you cannot consciously remember, but nevertheless they are affecting you today. If you even mildly suspect that this may be true, I would urge you to purchase their book.[1]

The Bible says, "Be angry, and do not sin: do not let the sun go down on your wrath" (Eph. 4:26). Anger is a natural response if someone or something has hurt you. Don't let anyone tell you that feeling angry isn't "Christian." Feeling angry is a normal part of the grieving process. But anger becomes a problem (or sin) when in time it leads to bitterness, resentment, and revenge. If in anger you take a stand against that which is wrong, you are expressing "Christian anger." If, however, you feel a desire for revenge, then you need to deal with your anger in a constructive way.

You can tell whether your anger is out of bounds if you deny restoration to the person who hurt you. Can you forgive the person who hurt you? Can you wish that person well? If not, you probably have a problem with anger.

If anger is a guiding force in your life, I would encourage you to do these four things:

1. Try to identify the true source of your anger. Is it really the boss who fired you, or perhaps someone in your past who hurt you as a child?
2. If you can identify the source of your anger, remind yourself that feeling angry is not wrong. You have the right to feel angry and to express it constructively.

3. Find ways to express your anger without giving in to actions that bring bitterness, resentment, or revenge. Begin to talk about your feelings with a professional counselor or at least a supportive friend who can listen and not pass judgment.

4. If your rage seems uncontrollable and you've been venting it on someone else (usually an innocent person—not the person with whom you're angry), try venting your anger on an object instead. When your anger rises, shut yourself in a room and allow yourself to cry and beat your fists on a pillow. It won't hurt the pillow, and you'll be able to physically vent your powerful emotions. Taking out your anger on an inanimate object is acceptable; venting it on a human being is not.

Don't expect that you'll be instantaneously freed from anger. The stages of grief are a process—one that takes time. There may be times during this process when you feel you've conquered your anger. Other times the anger may be suddenly triggered and you realize you must deal with it again. No one follows the exact same pattern and your situation is unique. Allow yourself all the time you need.

Bargaining

In the bargaining stage of grief you may still experience a feeling of unreality. Although you know consciously that your loss has taken place, you want to bargain for a different outcome. You may believe you are to blame for what happened and if you change yourself you will recover what you have lost.

A friend of my daughter, Donna Hartley, who also happens to be a professional Christian therapist, has seen many people in the bargaining stage of grief. She once said this to my daughter:

When we bargain, who do we bargain with? As Christians we bargain with God. Even non-Christians bargain with God or with "something." In this stage people set criteria for themselves. They say, "If I don't meet such-and-such conditions something bad will happen to me." If, for example, a friend commits suicide they may suffer tremendous guilt over not being able to prevent it. They may say, "I'm a terrible person because I couldn't help my friend. I can somehow redeem myself if I give up smoking cigarettes (or whatever they feel is their worse vice)." They feel if they just meet certain conditions their loss will be lessened or even reversed and they will somehow be worthy of forgiveness.[2]

Many Vietnam war veterans know about the bargaining stage of grief. Possibly they witnessed their army buddy's death and they feel they should have been able to save him. This feeling causes a guilt that can stay with a person forever.

Rhonda was a single mother who raised her son all by herself. Although Rhonda was a Christian woman who devoutly served the Lord, her son developed many problems in his teenage and young adult years. He had a history of drug and alcohol abuse as well as trouble with the law. As many mothers can identify, she felt responsible for his mistakes. Through the years she would bargain with God over her son's life. In her grief over his problems she would pray, "God, if you'll just help my son I'll never do anything wrong again."

While Rhonda's desire to do right was commendable, bargaining with God was wrong. When Rhonda's son eventually tried to commit suicide at the age of twenty-five, she was devastated. Since she had made a so-called bargain with God, she felt betrayed and abandoned. After a long time she began to realize the mistake she had made in trying to bargain with God.

Bargaining is one way for Satan to perpetrate one of his

favorite lies: You must earn forgiveness. In essence, Satan whispers in your ear and says, "God cannot forgive you unless you first become a 'good person.'" Waiting until we become "good enough" to merit God's forgiveness, we stay enmeshed and mired in our past hurts and mistakes.

In Psalm 51 King David is shattered and broken because he has had a one-night stand with a married woman, Bathsheba. To make matters worse, she gets pregnant. What does David do? He has her husband murdered. He then marries Bathsheba and thinks he has gotten away with his sin until Nathan, God's prophet, confronts him.

What is David's attitude? He says, "Wash me thoroughly from my iniquity, and cleanse me from my sin. For I acknowledge my transgressions, and my sin is ever before me" (Ps. 51:2–3).

David didn't bargain with God and say, "If You'll forgive me, I'll never do it again." He simply acknowledges his responsibility in the situation and asks for forgiveness.

The past is the past. Nothing can change it. When you make a mistake and suffer a loss because of it, God doesn't want you to torment yourself over it. You can begin the road to recovery by simply admitting your own responsibility and accepting God's forgiveness.

In 1 Timothy 1:13 Paul talks about his past: "Although I was formerly a blasphemer, a persecutor, and an insolent man . . . I obtained mercy because I did it ignorantly in unbelief. And the grace of our Lord was exceedingly abundant, with faith and love which are in Christ Jesus."

Paul could have looked back and said, "Why was I so bad? Why didn't I do something differently?" But instead he began to look at God's forgiveness.

Ultimately you are not responsible for another person's actions. You may have contributed to a problem or not felt a need, but you are not responsible for a choice and a decision someone else has made. In Rhonda's case she had to realize that her son's attempted suicide was not her decision but his, and no amount of bargaining was going to change it. Yes, it is natural to have deep sorrow for the past, for the wrongs you may have committed, but the memory of the past should not be allowed to cloud the sunshine of God's love and forgiveness. As someone once said, "God does not shoot His own wounded"—and neither does He put conditions on forgiveness.

When you finally come to the realization that despite all your efforts, despite all your "bargains," your loss cannot be reversed, you may have trouble with the next stage of grief: despair or depression.

Depression

One of the most difficult aspects of grief is the feeling of despair that often accompanies it. During this stage the yearning for what you have lost may be almost unbearable. You may feel hopeless and have difficulty functioning. You may lose your appetite, or conversely, find your solace in food. You may also become apathetic and withdraw from life.

My own depression during the time of my divorce was characterized by an appalling sinking feeling. I felt as if I were going down a roller coaster ride that never went up. Sometimes I would be lying on my bed and literally feel as if I were sinking right through the bed and the floor and into the earth. It was one of the most hellish experiences I've ever encountered.

There were many days when I felt I would never get better. At those times I would remember, and hold onto, comforting words I had read many years ago.

> In this sad world of ours, sorrow comes to all. Perfect relief is not possible, except with time. You cannot now realize that you will ever feel better. Is this not so? And yet it is a mistake. You are sure to be happy again. To

know this, which is certainly true will make you some
less miserable now. I have had experience enough to
know what I say.[3]

If you are in the pit of depression, you may think that
you will never feel better. If you get mired in self-pity, you
may feel you have no way out. It isn't necessarily wrong to
ask, "Why me?" but if you can't get past that question you
may be in trouble. The other side of the coin is, "Why not
you?" Who else would you want to put this on? Why should
you be excluded?

While visiting my parents during my crisis experience, I
shared with them the problems I was facing: my shattered
marriage, a lawsuit, an IRS audit, and a severely injured
ankle that temporarily kept me from fulfilling my speaking
engagements. Bursting into tears, I asked my father, "Why
me?"

He didn't answer me directly then, but about a week
later my father sent me this letter:

> Joanne, remember that God may have a thousand
> results in mind for one action. For example, in regard to
> your being hurt and falling . . . there may be several
> reasons that apply to you as to why you injured your
> ankle. Several unknown reasons why the church, at the
> last minute, was thrown back on its own resources when
> you couldn't show up, reasons why you were injured here
> in the city where your parents live . . . reasons why your
> own family was able to show you more love and concern
> than is possible in your own self-sufficient schedule, and
> on and on we could go if we could see the pattern of
> results from God's high position of insight.
>
> Sometimes you will be tempted to ask 'why?' Sometimes
> things are a result of our own frailties—like your hurt
> ankle, but some are the result of evil in man—such as the
> lawsuit and your marriage breakup. But, Joanne, they
> have all been permitted by God! Remember that.

God uses man's evil intentions to accomplish His purposes. Joseph said it right when he told his brothers, "You intended to harm me, but God intended it for good."

Yes, it is easy to get mired down in self-pity. Self-pity looks inward rather than outward or upward. There is a slogan about how we should handle our problems: Glance at your problems and gaze at God. We often do the opposite. When we are in depression, we often gaze at our problems and glance at God. If we'll just get our gaze on God we'll see that He is bigger than the problem.

If you are dealing with depression and can't seem to come out of it, sometimes there may be a medical reason. A chemical or hormonal imbalance may cause severe symptoms of depression. If you suspect this may be a problem, please consult with your doctor.

When you are deep in depression you may look at yourself and say, "I'm no good," but God looks at you and says, "I created you and I have plans for you." It doesn't matter how many mistakes you've made or what kind of loss you've experienced. God still has plans for you. Consequences? Yes, there will be consequences for sin, but that is not the end of life.

Depression can actually be a positive force in your life if it leads you to a place of brokenness before God with breaking of pride and self-sufficiency. God cannot use someone who says, "I can take care of myself. I'm self-made." We must come to realize that we should be dependent on God and His power in our lives.

Brokenness is the point when you acknowledge that God is sovereign and in control. You agree that He knows what is best for you, and therefore you are going to let Him work in your life. At this point He can really begin the restoration process in your situation.

What happens in your period of brokenness is your choice. Remember King David in Psalm 51? Not only did he ask God to forgive him, but he went on to say, "Create in me a clean heart, O God, and renew a steadfast spirit within me. Do not cast me away from Your presence, and do not take Your Holy Spirit from me" (Ps. 51:10–11). He could have said, "I've taken a man's wife and his life, my life is not valuable." Instead, he still had a heart for God and he knew that God loved him.

I think that everyone who has come through brokenness and out the other side has an overwhelming belief in God's love. No matter who they are, they just can't get away from God's love for them. I know this is certainly true in my life. The key is to work *through* the depression so that you *can* come out the other side.

Pastor Claude Robold of the New Covenant Church of God in Middletown, Ohio, has been a tremendous help in the research for this book. His wisdom, insight, and information has been invaluable. Pastor Robold relates the story of counseling two widows. The first woman was in her forties and had a grown daughter when her husband died. The second woman lost her husband at an even younger age and was left with three small children to raise.

After over three years of mourning, the first woman still has not come out of her depression. She is permeated with self-pity and frequently says, "I don't have any reason to live."

The second woman has dealt with her grief and depression in much less time and is getting on with the plan God has for her life. When asked what made the difference for her, she replied, "It comes down to a matter of choice. You either say, 'I'm going to be a joyful person through the power of God,' or 'I'm not.' I had to begin to act joyful even when I wasn't, because I had made a choice to be joyful. I stayed with that until God honored my commitment and brought real joy into my life."

The enemy, Satan, doesn't want you to rise above your

depression. As long as you are willing to sink into doom and gloom, despair or self-pity, he's right there. That's his graveyard and he'll keep watch over you. However, when there is joy, rejoicing, or praise, he can't handle it. The Lord inhabits praise and Satan has to leave.

It is up to you. At some point you've got to decide whether to stay in your depression or get on with your life. As I once heard, "You can go ahead and fall into a river and it won't hurt you at all. Staying in there is what will get you. You've got to get out!"

Feeling depressed is not the problem; that is a normal stage of grief. Staying depressed is what will get you. You've got to get out!

Acceptance/Adjustment

Reaching the acceptance/adjustment stage in the grief process is like coming out of a long, dark tunnel. In my own life I found I'd reached the acceptance stage when I could talk about my former husband in a normal tone of voice. I no longer felt the anger and despair that had once overwhelmed me.

Reaching the point of accepting your loss and going on with your life does not mean that you will never again feel remorse or sadness. Although I'm making a new life for myself, I still have times when I cry and feel sorrow about my first husband and the loss of our relationship. I'm sure this sadness about my loss will stay with me forever, but I've learned that this is part of the grieving process too.

Adjusting to your loss means that you can pick up the pieces and begin to start anew. There may still be times, however, when you are once again overwhelmed by grief. When this happens you may have to work through the stages again, but usually much more quickly. You may find yourself dealing with only one of the stages of grief—anger, for example—and you'll only need to work through that stage again. With the complexity of human nature and the diversity of the losses we experience there is no way to predict exactly your reaction. A friend of mine, Maggie, has learned to see such sudden emotional flashbacks as a normal response to her loss, rather than a sign of unresolved grief.

Maggie had a childhood no one would envy. While in the fourth grade Maggie's mother was involved in a near-fatal car accident. Although it happened over thirty years ago, the events are still vivid in Maggie's mind. "I remember being in school when a police officer came to tell me my mother was at the hospital. Since my father had died when I was a baby and my mother was now in a coma, I had no one who could help me and give me the emotional support I needed. My older sister and I were separated and put into different foster homes. For the next three years I rarely saw my mother or sister. I was in limbo."

Maggie's foster family treated her well but since she was with them only "temporarily" she never felt totally accepted. After three long years her mother was finally released from the hospital and reunited with her family, but nothing was ever the same again. Her mother still required frequent hospitalizations, and they moved to another city away from any friends she had made.

During her adolescence Maggie began the process of grieving for the many losses she had sustained, and as an adult she was eventually able to put her past into perspective. She has since raised a family and has been able to use her life story to help other hurting people. Most of the time she can remember and deal with her past impartially. She has worked through her grief and can now see how God has used her life and brought about good through her experiences.

Nevertheless, Maggie occasionally has times when her past hurts come cascading into her memory and she finds herself weeping. This usually happens when she is counseling or sharing with another hurting person, and the Lord brings these memories to the forefront. Maggie has learned that these memories can still hold pain, but she also knows that she has dealt with her real grief and these flashbacks are brief. The emotional response does not mean that she has unresolved grief, but that old hurt and pain can wash over her when she is vulnerable.

In my own life I've had a similar experience. Whenever I'm leading a seminar and I get to the session on forgiveness I usually start to cry. During this session I share with women attendees about my divorce and the other crisis situations I've experienced. I have great difficulty talking about and reliving a very painful time in my life, but I've learned to accept that this, too, is a part of the grieving process.

Working through your own grief does not mean that you will be forever free from pain and old memories. Remember, it is a process. You won't go to sleep one night and wake up the next morning with the sudden revelation that you are no longer grieving. The feeling may sneak up on you slowly with a gentle, growing awareness that you are healing.

When you break a bone you don't suddenly find that one day the bone is healed. Instead, it is in the process of mending a little bit every day. Just as our physical breaks take time to heal, so do our emotional ones.

At some point you will realize that you are no longer actively grieving. You'll be able to look ahead and give tomorrow a chance. You'll be ready to truly start over again.

FORGIVENESS:
When You Feel That You've Failed

Mark it—when God forgives, He forgets.
He is not only willing, but pleased to use any vessel—
just as long as it is clean today.
It may be cracked or chipped.
It may be worn or it may have never been used before.
You can count on this—the past ended one second ago.
From this point onward, you can be clean,
filled with His spirit,
and used in many different ways for His honor.

—Charles R. Swindoll, *Starting Over*[1]

CHAPTER THREE

The letter was left lying on my desk with all of the other mail for that day. I had just rushed into my office on my way to another appointment, so I quickly scanned through the stack of envelopes. I figured I'd take time to read them later that afternoon, but for some reason one envelope grabbed my attention. Although I didn't recognize the return address, I decided to take the time to open it.

Inside the envelope was a beautiful letter about forgiveness from a woman I've never met, but one that I'll never forget. You see, she wrote from her prison cell in Gatesville, Texas, and this is what she had to say:

Dear Joanne,

I was listening to the program "Focus on the Family" the day of your interview. I accepted the Lord three years ago, but it wasn't until a couple of years ago that I surrendered to Him. Although I am young in the Lord, I've grown by leaps and bounds. I've been set free in many areas of my life.

One of those areas of freedom is from the bondage and shame of being sexually abused by my father. My whole life revolved around that. I hated him and blamed myself for many years.

As a result, my self-esteem was extremely low. I need not expound on the gutter life-style I led. Needless to say, I was capable of anything. But not with the intention to shift all the blame, because at a certain point I was responsible for the choices and course I took.

My incarceration and crimes (I am here for shooting and murdering my husband) are direct consequences of those choices. But, praise God, I am now a new creation in Christ Jesus.

One of the principal steps I took was to forgive my father and myself. I am grateful for taking that step because four months after the amends were made, my father died in a car wreck. Praise God, we are at peace today.

Since that time, things started unraveling for me. My life has changed dramatically (my attitude, thoughts, and love for other people). In and through that decision [to forgive] and God's power, I'm taking daily steps to improve myself spiritually, physically, and mentally.

I feel like a light in a dark, desolate place. I should say, an instrument of peace! Because this place can be as bright as you make it. I am grateful for the bright peace and freedom I have. I realize to grow I must give it away . . . .

This letter brings me renewed hope. This woman has found the peace that comes through forgiveness. It doesn't matter what terrible, tragic sin she committed, God's forgiveness is available to her—and to you too.

You may have a moral charge against you or a criminal record. You may have been an abuser in an abusive situation. Possibly you are haunted by memories of an illicit, adulterous, or homosexual relationship. You may be financially bankrupt or strangling in the clutches of a terrible habit. Maybe you've gotten a divorce, had an abortion, or been responsible for damaging another person's life. Now you feel that you're a worthless failure.

You don't need to continue feeling this way. I have

learned that the negative circumstances and problems in life don't have to be devastating. Instead, they can become possibilities for new service to God and others. Failure is not final—it is often the door to starting over again. Forgiveness is the key to opening that door.

Sadly, Christians often want to classify sins. We think that some sins can be forgiven, while others cannot, but this is not what the Bible says! In God's eyes sin is sin— there is not one sin that is worse than another. No matter what you've done, no matter what sin has been committed, God wants to forgive you.

In Sunday school, little children are taught the song, "Jesus Loves Me." One of the verses says: "Jesus loves me when I'm good, when I do the things I should."

For many of us that is where the verse ends. We've forgotten that the rest of the verse says: "Jesus loves me when I'm bad, even though it makes Him sad."

It's time we all learned the truth of the last part of that verse: God's love and forgiveness extend to you, regardless of your mistakes.

Accepting God's Forgiveness

While going through my crisis experience I was often incapacitated by feelings of guilt. For two years after my divorce I was haunted by my "if onlys." I'd torture myself by thinking, *If only I'd paid more attention to my husband's needs.* Or, *If only I'd insisted on marriage counseling earlier.* Hardly a day went by that I didn't feel extreme guilt over all the things I realized in hindsight I should have done.

Since my former husband was very athletic and a sports enthusiast, my guilt trips centered on the fact that I hadn't shared this enthusiasm. During our marriage, if he was playing church league basketball or softball, I rarely participated in the events even as a spectator. After the divorce I learned that one of the biggest needs in a man's life is that his wife be involved in his leisure activities. I learned this fact too late. Since I hadn't fulfilled this need in my husband's life, I tormented myself with accusations that fueled my guilt. Longing to be free from the guilt, I realized that I couldn't be free until I learned to forgive myself for past mistakes.

Part of forgiving myself included the realization that true forgiveness originates with God. As a human being I will fail at some point or another. Since I'm not perfect, forgiveness cannot start with me; it must come first through God.

If you're struggling with guilt and want to be free from it, the first step is to receive God's forgiveness for your past hurts, mistakes, and sins. It's not difficult. Receiving God's forgiveness requires only one thing: that you confess your sin before Him.

First John 1:9 says, "If we confess our sins, He is faithful and just to forgive us our sins and to cleanse us from all unrighteousness." Christians often quote this verse to someone who wants to accept Jesus Christ as his Savior, but it is also a written guarantee to Christians that if they confess, God *will* forgive.

The word *cleanse* in this verse comes from the original Greek word *catharsis,* which means a release or a relief from burdens. God's catharsis or cleansing brings relief.

I found great relief for my own feelings of guilt about my failed marriage when I was finally able to confess all my past mistakes and sins. Confession brought relief even for the sins of omission—like not attending my husband's sporting events—and I was free at last from guilt about my "if onlys."

Unconfessed sin saps vitality, affecting a person physically, emotionally, and spiritually. Physically, it will induce depression and irritability since physical strength and resources are depleted by leading a double life. Emotionally, unconfessed sin fills you with fear and anger. Spiritually, you're burdened with guilt. The only way to be restored physically, emotionally, and spiritually is to confess your sin and ask to be forgiven.

In my seminars I always try to provide an opportunity for hurting women to find this restoration. Without it, life's burdens can become unbearable. I'd like to provide the same opportunity for you today.

First, find time to be completely alone with no distractions. Take along a piece of paper and a pen. This is not a game or a fun exercise, but a way for you to enter into the very presence of the Lord.

As you begin, ask the Holy Spirit to come into the room and envelop you with His love and comfort. Listen as you hear the Lord's footsteps at your heart's door. Picture the door opening as you gaze into a familiar face—the face of Jesus. He has come looking just for you.

As you invite Him in, He sits down close beside you. His eyes are full of compassion as you begin to speak. Now is your chance to say to Him, "Oh, Lord, I have sinned . . . ."

- There is something so shameful I've never been able to tell anyone . . . .

- There is something so petty that keeps coming up over and over . . . .

- There is an error, something I was supposed to do and didn't. An error of omission . . . .

- I didn't speak in love as I should have . . . .

Whatever you need to confess, just let the words come out. Imagine that as you are speaking, Jesus turns to embrace you. You hear Him say, "I forgive you" as you feel all the malice, anger, hatred, bitterness, jealousy, shame, fear, and condemnation being taken from you. He is cleansing you and giving you relief.

Now take that piece of paper and write down your confession. Write, "Oh, Lord, I have sinned . . ." and name your sins. After you've done this, write, "Forgive me, I pray." Hold that piece of paper in your hand and realize that Christ is near. When you pray for forgiveness, God hears you and takes the sin from you. The Scriptures say that when we confess, God forgives, and when God forgives, sin is absolutely obliterated from His memory. (See Isa. 43:25 and Heb. 8:12)

As a symbol of God taking that sin away from you, allow yourself to *hear* God's forgiveness. Take that paper in both hands and tear it up. What a sweet, sweet sound. You are forgiven!

Over and over again I've seen women's lives reborn as they allowed themselves to experience God's forgiveness in this way. A few months ago, for instance, I was in Bellingham, Washington, for a seminar. At the end of the session on forgiveness I gave the women an opportunity to participate in this exercise. They were able to write down their sin, confess it, and then tear up the paper.

After the session a dear woman who felt clean and forgiven for the first time came up and said: "When I first came here my face had a deep frown and the corners of my mouth were turned downward. I could feel all the tenseness in my face. As I confessed my sin, asked to be forgiven, and tore up the piece of paper, my face completely lightened. My frown was not able to stay and it was like I had no control to do anything but smile. I know you asked us to keep our eyes closed in prayer but I had to lift my head and let the smile come out. I have never experienced this before. Thank God, I feel so released and peaceful!"

Letting Go of Your Past

After you've confessed your sin, written it down, and torn up the paper, the next step is to paste the pieces of paper back together again and carry the paper around in your wallet the rest of your life, right? Wrong! The next step is to throw it away—get rid of it!

We all have things in our lives that we hope no one will ever find out. We all have skeletons that need burying, but we leave them hanging in our closets instead so we can continually check on them! It's time to clean out the closets! God's forgiveness works in vain when you refuse to bury the skeletons of past mistakes.

Dr. Gordon McMinn, a Christian psychologist, once wrote: "There appear to be two benefits from looking back. The first value comes from seeing things differently, thus hurts and misunderstandings can be healed by new insight. A second benefit in reviewing the past is to gain information that provides wisdom to act on now and in the future. Healing and learning, in my opinion, provide the only incentive for personal reflection."[2]

The past should *only* be reflected upon for your benefit. Sadly, most people who concentrate on their past mistakes reap no benefits at all. Instead of learning from, or receiving healing for their mistakes, those mistakes haunt their present and stop them from forgiving themselves. By concentrating on their past, these people accomplish only one thing: failure in the present.

A few months ago at one of my seminars, a woman came up to me with tears in her eyes and told me this sad story:

> For thirteen years I had a wonderful best friend. We went through many of life's ups and downs, helped raise each other's children, and often confided in each other. Three

years ago we got caught up in a petty argument that grew into something larger. Our friendship was ruined and we never spoke to each other again. Last year my friend died. I really miss her and keep wondering why I couldn't let our past differences go.

Contrast this story with what a smiling and cheerful woman shared with me a few weeks later:

All my life I grew up knowing that my parents didn't want me. When I was conceived my parents weren't married and because of me they had to elope. Although my parents were both Christians, my mother and father never had a happy marriage and my mother blamed me. There were many times when she would say, "If I could do it over again, I would have an abortion." In essence, she wished I'd never been born.

In my childhood I felt that if I were only prettier, smarter, or nicer my mother would want me. When I grew up, I had to learn to forgive myself for not being perfect, so that I could then forgive my mother. Today I feel no bitterness or anger toward her because I was able to put the past behind me. God has a plan and a purpose for my life. I can't let the pain from my past cloud the joy of my present.

As these two different stories illustrate, accepting God's forgiveness is only the first step. You've got to learn to forgive yourself and let go of your past.

For a long time I could not even think about my former husband without an extreme emotional response, and since I was always thinking about him, this caused a lot of problems. For months I vacillated between extreme anger, where I placed all the blame on him, and extreme guilt, where I placed all the blame on myself. When I felt guilty I couldn't believe God would ever use me for His glory again. When I felt angry, I knew God could not use me as I was at that point. Either way, I felt defeated. During this time a good friend of mine, Pastor Monte Knudsen, wrote to me: "Never let the enemy feed you his lies of condemnation. When you read about the heroes of faith in Hebrews 11, none of their mistakes are mentioned—only their faith and victories. God forever forgets our past and takes us to new heights of freedom and joy when *we* release our past." What a wonderful message of hope Monte sent to me! I'll always be grateful to him for those encouraging words.

True, we can never forgive and forget the way that God does. But we can *choose* to release our past and live our lives in the present. What keeps us from releasing our past? Most of the time we're bound by feelings of guilt.

Dealing with Guilt

When we sin we break God's moral laws. His laws are non-negotiable. When we violate His standards, consequences result. Some sins are more visible, some have more consequences, but all of them have the ability to produce feelings of guilt. Forgiveness requires not only letting go of your past, but also letting go of the guilt associated with it.

Invariably, people who are burdened with guilt are the ones who criticize and point a finger at other people's sins and inadequacies. They think that by pointing out someone else's failure they will take the spotlight off their own mistakes.

Guilt is a real problem. Unless you deal with it, you can't develop normally and become spiritually healthy. Guilt blocks your relationship with God and is the root of many problems. And guilt will not simply go away. In Acts 24:16, Paul writes: "I myself always strive to have a conscience without offense toward God and men." Notice that Paul says he *strives* to have a clear conscience. A guilt-free life doesn't happen by accident. It takes an understanding of what is causing your guilt: is it from God or Satan?

In the middle of my crisis I was involved in weekly counseling sessions with a wonderful Christian psychologist, Dr. Larry Day. During the course of our sessions I revealed to him portions of my childhood. In particular one instance stands out as significant to my healing process. I told him about the vivid memory I have of being thirteen years old and attending our church's annual camp meeting. Following an evening service I went forward to the altar to accept Jesus Christ as my Savior. It sounds like a lovely story, doesn't it?

I only wish it were. You see, it was not my first or even my second trip to the altar for the exact same reason. Year after year, service after service, I'd go forward to the altar because I didn't always "feel" like a Christian. The church that I attended placed a great deal of emphasis on performance, or being "good enough" to be saved. Since I felt I had made a lot of mistakes, I was always feeling guilty, and I could never feel good enough. I had the mistaken idea that I was never completely forgiven.

Dr. Day helped me to finally put that part of my past into perspective when he said, "I wish I could have been there so I could have lifted you up from the altar, looked into your child eyes, and said, 'No more, no more, Joanne. It's already done. You are forgiven. You're a child of God. Now believe it.'"

Two Types of Guilt

For too many years I carried around a huge load of guilt about things I'd already confessed before the Lord. Not until adulthood did I learn that there are *two* kinds of guilt—one from God and the other from Satan. *Justified* guilt is true guilt from God; *unjustified* guilt is false guilt from Satan. What a revelation that was to me. Now, through knowledge and understanding I've been able to experience new freedom in this area.

Justified Guilt

Justified guilt convicts us of our sins and prompts us to repentance. As a positive force it leads us to deal with unrealized and unconfessed sin. Justified guilt, present from the very first sin committed by Adam and Eve, is characterized by two things: a desire to run away and hide from God, and a desire to blame someone else for our sin. Justified guilt tells us that we're not right with God.

Small children are some of the best examples of this type of guilt. My grandson, Jameson, knows about justified guilt. He has accepted Jesus as his Savior and really wants to do what is right. Last year, when he was five years old, he started kindergarten. In class with him was a boy named Joshua. Jameson and Joshua didn't get along. One day Jameson came home telling his mom about this "mean boy Joshua" who was always taking Jameson's crayons and throwing sand at him on the playground. Deanna said to him, "Does Joshua have any friends?"

To which Jameson replied, "No, because no one likes him."

"Don't you think Joshua is probably pretty lonely?"

"Well, I don't know. Everytime I see him he is playing by himself."

"That's because he doesn't have any friends and that makes him feel sad and angry. Maybe you could help him by being friends with him."

"Hmmm . . . that's a good idea. I think I'll maybe try playing with him tomorrow."

Feeling good about Jameson's response and believing that the situation was settled, Deanna didn't think too much about it until one afternoon when Jameson came home from school and went straight to his room without a word. Normally a gregarious and talkative child, his mother called him out of his room to find out what was wrong. "Nothing," said Jameson as he looked at the floor and scuffed his toes.

"Are you feeling okay?" asked his mom.

"Yes, but I want to be alone," he said.

Puzzled by his strange behavior, Deanna was about to press the issue when the telephone rang. As Deanna went to answer it, Jameson went back to his room. The phone call was from Jameson's teacher saying that Jameson had been in a fight at school. With whom? You guessed it. Joshua. After talking with the teacher, it was clear why Jameson had been acting in such a strange manner. He felt guilty!

When Deanna went to talk with Jameson she knew what to ask. The conversation went something like this:

"Jameson, did you get in a fight with Joshua today?"

"No."

"Jameson, your teacher just called me and told me about it."

"Joshua started it! He just came up and pushed me!"

"Did that mean you had to push him back?"

"He's always bothering me!"

"Is that why you hit him?"

"I didn't start it!"

Plainly even at age five, Jameson exhibited the symptoms of a guilty conscience. His first reaction was to hide in his room and not to let anyone see him. His second reaction was to blame someone else.

As Deanna continued to talk with Jameson he was finally able to admit that he had done the wrong thing. Once he was able to admit it, he began to cry. At that point he could say, "I'm sorry," and be forgiven. Immediately he was ready to run outside and play. He started talking and laughing with much animation—just like his old self. In fact, he couldn't wait until the next day at school so that he could apologize to his teacher and to Joshua. From that day on, he and Joshua were friends.

Jameson's story illustrates one of the key principles of recognizing justified guilt. When the guilt is justified it *disappears* after you've confessed your sin and asked to be forgiven. For Jameson, it didn't mean that the fight with Joshua had never happened. But after confessing it, he could go on from that moment free of guilt. Jameson didn't let his past mistake cloud his future. He didn't go around for months afterward saying, "I should never have gotten into that fight. Now no one will ever like me. I'm not worthy to have any friends." That would seem pretty ridiculous, wouldn't it? So why do we continually remind ourselves about our own failures? Why do we burden ourselves with guilt that lasts for months and years, when in fact we've already asked for and received God's forgiveness?

Unjustified Guilt

If you're still feeling guilty after you've confessed your sin before God and asked His forgiveness, it's not justified guilt. Instead you're dealing with unjustified guilt that comes through Satan. Since God has dismissed from His memory every sin that is brought before Him by a repentant heart, guilt over confessed sin cannot be from Him. Instead, it is Satan who accuses us. Since he can't rob us of our salvation through Jesus Christ, he settles for robbing us of the joy of that salvation by getting us to concentrate on our failures. That's why Paul wrote in Philippians 3:13, "Brethren, I do not count myself to have apprehended; but one thing I do, forgetting those things which are behind and reaching forward to those things which are ahead."

At every one of my seminars I meet women who are still looking back and not reaching forward. They are struggling with the problems of unjustified guilt. Although they recognize that through Jesus Christ they are forgiven, they can't forgive themselves. All their lives they've carried feelings of guilt and inadequacy. Possibly you can identify with what a few of the women have shared with me.

- I need prayer for deep inner healing. My mom is an alcoholic. My father physically abused me. I have forgiven them but still am affected in areas of my emotions. I am also a recovering alcoholic. My husband is helping me through this, but I can't seem to forgive myself.

- I hurt so bad, but I really can't tell you why—I don't know! It probably goes back to a divorce after twenty-five years—then he *died*—we have two children. I think I can't forgive myself because I failed.

- Three years ago my son was seriously burned. Since that time Satan has continually told me it was my fault and that I was a bad mother. During the past three years I have dealt with some of it, but it has affected my relationship with God and my daughter. She feels rejected because I paid more attention to my son.

One of Satan's favorite weapons is to make us feel unjustified guilt for past mistakes, causing us to believe that we can never start over after we've made a mistake and failed. Satan is our accuser—he accuses our conscience of sins that have already been dismissed from God's mind. Satan arouses our feelings of guilt to make us believe that we're worthless and don't deserve a second chance. We don't realize that God uses our shortcomings and our failures, just as He uses our talents and virtues.

I love the story about Tom Watson, president of the IBM Corporation, who called an employee into his office one day. This particular employee, through a large mistake, had just cost the company one million dollars! Of course the employee knew he'd been called into the president's office to be fired, but after Tom Watson was finished talking to him, Mr. Watson said, "Okay. That's it! Now back to work!"

Totally stunned, the employee stammered, "But, aren't you going to fire me?"

Mr. Watson replied, "Fire you? We've just spent one million dollars *educating* you!"

God is like that. He stays with us through our failures, no matter what. He uses our mistakes to *educate* us and make us richer for our education. With Him, we always have a second chance. Often we miss this very important fact because we're still burdened with unjustified guilt.

One way that we receive unjustified guilt is by acquiring it. In this situation someone else heaps the guilt on us and we accept it. This happens when another person convinces you that you're at fault, even though God has forgiven you.

In my experience guilt brings a mountain of pain. Just a few months ago I prayed, "Oh, dear God, I hurt today so very much. Help me. Ease the pain inside me." I was in emotional pain because someone else had tried to accuse me. I made a telephone call to a pastor who was interested in scheduling me to come to his church for a seminar. As always, I explained to him about my divorce. He then started in on a series of very personal questions which were extremely painful to answer. He continued to tell me his views about divorce. His words were cruel and cut open old wounds. I began to feel as if I was suffocating, but as I listened to his diatribe I silently prayed, "Oh, Lord, You are my source. You have my whole future in Your hands. Please help me now to keep my attitude Christlike."

I finally broke into his accusations and said as gently as I could, "Listen, I don't think there is any point in continuing this conversation. The past is the past. I cannot relive or redo it. I believe in forgiveness and know that God is not finished with me yet. I believe in restoration. I've had a hard struggle to start over and I'm not going to quit now."

In effect that ended our conversation and as I hung up the phone I was reminded of my former pastor, Tom

Wilson, when he said to me, "You've felt enough loss and rejection. You wouldn't want to go to a church where you might receive more rejection. Go only where you'll have the freedom to minister as God would have you." Much to my amazement, that same pastor called me back a few weeks later and scheduled a seminar!

In certain cases you may acquire guilt even when you haven't done anything wrong. This is the case with spouses whose mates are involved in adulterous relationships.

When Marie's husband left her for another woman Marie was crushed. She had no idea that her husband was cheating on her. The night she discovered the truth she thought she must be going crazy. Learning of her husband's infidelity she felt a compelling urge to take a shower. She went into the bathroom, undressed, and let the warm water run over her body. After a vigorous scrubbing she still felt she wasn't clean. Even after finishing the shower she felt as though dirt was caked on her skin.

That night after crying herself to sleep in an empty bed, Marie woke up in a sweat. She had been dreaming that black dirt was burying her. In her dream she struggled to be rid of the dirt and even tried to peel her skin off. No matter how many layers of skin she peeled she was not able to be free. She then began tearing her skin off in chunks and it still didn't help. Upon awakening she was so terrified she didn't dare go back to sleep again.

As soon as she could the next morning she called her professional Christian counselor and told him what had happened. He explained to her that often when a person is wronged, he or she experiences these overwhelming feelings of guilt. Just as though Marie had been raped, it was an attack and an invasion of her mind and spirit. Once she could understand that this was a normal reaction to a traumatic experience she was able to rest and find a measure of peace.

As with accrued guilt you've got to refuse to accept guilt

heaped on you by someone else. Just refuse to take it on. This may take working on your self-esteem, but before you're finished reading this book I hope you'll have enough knowledge and insight to really let go of the guilt.

When unjustified guilt assails us, we need to be able to claim 1 John 3:20: "For if our heart condemns us, God is greater than our heart, and knows all things." When Satan tries to accuse us before God, he can't get anywhere because "we have an Advocate with the Father, Jesus Christ the righteous" (1 John 2:1). If Satan can't get anywhere when he accuses us before God, we can use the same defense. Silence the accuser by claiming the power of Jesus. When confronted with the reality of the shed blood of Christ, Satan has to flee. Use it as your shield when feelings of guilt attack you. Remember, every sin that is confessed before God is covered by the blood of Christ, your best defense against an attack of unjustified guilt.

Learning to Say "I'm Sorry"

After we've asked for God's forgiveness, it is sometimes necessary to ask for another person's forgiveness. For most of us this is an unpleasant task. We don't like to admit that we were wrong; it goes against our human nature. But a true apology can bring restoration in broken relationships.

In fact, I've learned that the best way to say "I'm sorry" is to ask the question, "Will you forgive me?" Saying, "I'm sorry" does not require a response; "Will you forgive me?" does.

I remember when I was involved in the divorce recovery workshops. During one particularly difficult session on forgiveness, Pastor Steve Bearden said, "There will come a day, even if you were not the person seeking a divorce, when you must say to your former spouse, 'Will you forgive me for the things that I knowingly and unknowingly did to be a part of this breakup?" It may take you twenty years, but at some point it must be done so that the process of forgiveness can be complete."

At that moment I thought to myself, "I'll take the twenty years!" Pastor Steve shared with us, "*Every* person who gets a divorce feels that it is the other person's fault!"

Several times that night Pastor Steve said that we should not wait until the other person apologizes first. In fact, even expecting an apology in return was the wrong attitude. We are only responsible for our actions. We're not responsible for how someone else responds.

I went home that night full of mixed feelings. I didn't know if I'd ever be able to ask for forgiveness from my former husband. I had to put the idea on the shelf for a while and allow myself time to heal. I really thought it could take twenty years!

To my surprise, several months later, I received a phone call from my former husband. I had done a lot of healing during those months and in my heart I could hear the Lord nudging me, saying "now." So, with a trembling voice and tears running down my face, I said, "Will you forgive me for the things that I knowingly and unknowingly did to be a part of our breakup?"

As I said the words a peace enveloped me. I felt sweet release and a sense of well-being. As my former husband accepted my apology, I realized that the apology was for *me*. I was the one who needed to feel the peace and the release of anger and resentment.

Saying "I'm sorry" benefits you more than it benefits the offended person. Not only do you grow by acknowledging your responsibility, you have the personal satisfaction and peace that comes from doing the right thing. It's not true that "Love means you never have to say you're sorry." Love *requires* that you say you're sorry.

FORGIVENESS:
When Someone Else Has Failed You

The cure for all the ills and wrongs,
the cares, the sorrows, and the crimes of humanity,
all lie in the one word love.
It is the divine vitality
that everywhere produces and restores life.

—Lydia Maria Child

CHAPTER FOUR

Someone has hurt you, perhaps yesterday or many years ago, and you are still feeling the pain. You are not alone. Almost everyone has experienced deep hurt from the past that carries over into the present. One of my deepest hurts comes from childhood and still affects me today.

As a child I was very vivacious, outgoing, and spirited. In comparison my brother and sisters seemed quiet, reserved, and shy. I often heard comments like, "Well, we know who the black sheep of this family is." Or, "If there is ever a problem, you can be sure Joanne is behind it." Somehow I grew up with the mistaken idea that there was something wrong with my natural vivacity.

A couple of years ago my mother told me that when I was very small and needed to be quiet (in church for example), my father was the only one who could keep me still. He had to physically restrain me and hold me still on his lap. My earliest memory is that my father was restraining me. I felt my father's disapproval, and I believed I could never please him.

My feelings of inadequacy were compounded by the fact that, as I remember it, my family didn't express love with large doses of hugs, kisses, and verbal affirmations. Although I knew my parents loved me, and I feel they did the best they could with the knowledge they had from their own upbringing, I was raised during a time when expressing love verbally and physically was not considered as important as it is today.

I desperately wanted my father's love and acceptance, but I was boisterous and playful, not shy and soft-spoken. Since I didn't know how to change my personality, I tried inappropriate ways to gain his approval.

As the years passed I cried out for attention. When I was fourteen, I even made up an unknown assailant. One night when I had gone to the corner mailbox to mail a letter, I let my active imagination run wild as I walked back home. It was early evening, but already dark outside. Somehow the idea just grew within me and by the time I reached home I burst through the door, crying that a man was chasing me and had tried to attack me. Of course this caused a big commotion and my father *had* to pay attention to me. To my delight, he ran outside looking for the man! To my utter surprise he believed me!

My father was so protective and caring that I felt obligated to further the deception. I went as far as going with my father to fill out a police report. In my need for attention I let my conscience take a back seat.

That night I felt for the first time that I really had my father's full attention, but I hadn't counted on not being able to live with my own lies. The next day the guilt was unbearable, and I had to go to my father and confess that I had made up the whole story. Admitting my lies was a relief but also a humiliation because my father made me go to the police station and apologize. The police were understanding and tolerant of a young girl's made-up story, but the whole experience taught me it was better to be honest. However, my need to be the apple of my father's eye was left unsatisfied. Although my honesty was rewarded by a clear conscience, I still ached to win my father's love and approval.

One summer when I was sixteen and my family was

attending our church's annual camp meeting, I got caught holding hands with a boy. My dad wanted to talk to me about this, and so he took me on a walk around the campgrounds. The whole time we were walking and he was scolding me, he had his arm around my shoulder. It felt like heaven! I remember thinking, *I don't care how angry you are, or how much you scold me, I'll do anything for you if you'll just put your arm around me and touch me more.*

This hunger for my father's love has carried over into adulthood. I think it could be one of the reasons why I first began a public speaking career. Somehow a small part of me felt that if other people wanted to hear what I had to say, then maybe my father would notice and give his approval as well.

The hunger I have for my father's love came out verbally when I had to confront my parents with the tragic news that my marriage was ending in divorce. I drove several hours to their home and cried almost the whole way there. All of my past failures came back to haunt me and I dreaded having to tell them about the worst one of all.

As I came through my parents' front door all the years of feeling inadequate rushed to the forefront. Sobbing, I turned to my father and blurted out, "Well, I've blown it again!" Still weeping, I continued, "I don't feel I've ever done *anything* to please you." Expecting him to accept my outburst with his usual reserve, I was overwhelmed to find that he actually put his arm around me to comfort me. Years of pain started to fade as I heard him say, "It's okay." As I continued to sob and he held me, I felt that he was crying with me. I could feel that his back was damp with perspiration, as if his whole body was weeping.

Three times that evening I heard my father say, "I love you." My father was accepting me, faults and all! My heart began a new healing, although it wasn't the end of the pain.

Old habits don't die easily, and in the ensuing months

and years my father has sometimes slipped back into his reserved ways. At times I find myself dealing with the pain of rejection, but I now know it is not entirely my fault or my father's fault. I've had to learn to accept that I must be the first one to say "I love you" to him, and that it is enough that his answer is "Me, too."

Although I may wish that parts of my upbringing had been different, I know that I now have a choice to make about my own life. I must not blame my parents and use them as an excuse for wrong attitudes or behavior.

If you've been putting all the blame on someone else you may be wise to remember this fact: *You have the choice to make a change.* This does not mean that people won't hurt you and cause you deep pain; it simply means that you can stop *blaming* them. Anytime you are hurt by other people, the tendency is to focus your anger, grief, and resentment on them. By blaming them and focusing on them, you are surrendering your life to them. When you allow yourself to surrender to anger, grief, and resentment, their wrong behavior creates wrong behavior in you.

Are You Ready to Forgive?

When someone has hurt you, you may not be capable of forgiving him or her immediately. Forgiveness takes time.

If you watched the 1984 Olympics held in Los Angeles you probably saw an example of someone not being ready to forgive. Mary Decker had trained for years for a race that lasted only minutes. She had even put off marriage so that she could concentrate on winning that race. Her whole purpose and dedication was to get the gold medal.

Zola Budd admired Mary Decker. Zola also trained and worked so that she could compete in the race. She too wanted the gold medal.

As you may recall, during that crucial race, Zola tried to cross into Mary's lane to take the lead. In the process she caused Mary to break her stride and actually stumble on Zola's back leg. Mary then fell to the inside track, her hopes of winning the race gone.

Do you know what happened after the race? Zola Budd went over to apologize to Mary Decker, but Mary was not ready to forgive. She was still in shock; she needed time to get herself back together before she could say, "I forgive you."

Many times as Christians we are told to forgive immediately. We are taught to act like it didn't happen. "Forgive, forget, and get on with life," we're told. I've found that deep hurts take time to heal and that forgiveness is a process. Mary Decker needed more than seconds to be able to forgive. She needed more time than the end of the race or a few days. It was months before Mary Decker could answer in a letter to Zola Budd and say, "It's okay."

As Christians we want to throw Scripture verses at people like, "Forgive others as Christ has forgiven you" (see Col. 3:13). Yes, we are to forgive others as Christ has forgiven us, but sometimes this forgiveness takes time. Forgiving, just like grieving, is a process.

Tom and Katherine were married for over fifteen years. Both were committed Christians and through most of those years they enjoyed a happy and stable marriage. Although they had weathered some difficult times, Katherine believed that Tom would never have an affair with another woman.

One evening over dinner Tom smashed her belief by admitting to an affair with one of Katherine's closest friends, Maureen. To Katherine, the unbelievable was happening and she went into a state of shock. Although she was still functioning in the real world, her mind could not assimilate the fact that Tom had been unfaithful to her.

Just three days later Katherine received a phone call from one of the pastors at her church. Maureen had gone to this pastor to confess her affair with Tom. Now the pastor wanted to bring Maureen over to ask Katherine's forgiveness.

At first Katherine felt very angry. She told the pastor that she didn't feel like forgiving Maureen. She explained that she still could not truly believe that Maureen and Tom had had an affair.

Her pastor, not realizing or seeming to care about Katherine's pain, began to quote scriptures to Katherine about how she had to forgive Maureen *now*. Finally, Katherine gave in to his pressure. She said, "Okay, if you say I must do it, I will. But I will only say it with my mouth because I do not feel it in my heart yet. Maybe in time God can heal my heart and then I can really mean it."

Her pastor accepted her statement and told her he was bringing Maureen by her house that very evening. When Maureen arrived with the pastor, she sat down opposite Katherine and said, "Will you forgive me?"

Feeling like a robot, Katherine said, "Because I am a Christian I guess I must say it, but I want you to know that I don't feel it at all. I hope someday I can really feel it and mean it. With my mouth I'll say 'Yes, I forgive you.'"

Looking back at that moment, Katherine remembers, "I almost threw up all over my plush carpet. I started to sweat and felt as if a huge weight was pushing down on my shoulders. I barely recall the pastor praying with me before he and Maureen left."

Katherine never saw Maureen again. To this day, years later, she still struggles with her feelings about Maureen.

Katherine was forced to try and forgive before she was ready. She should have been allowed time to heal before Maureen confronted her. Forced forgiveness is not true forgiveness. Out of the flesh, you can *say* you're going to forgive, just as Katherine did, but you can't truly forgive without allowing God's spirit to live in and through you.

A desire to smooth things over encourages forced forgiveness in which hurt feelings are put aside, *but not re-*

solved. You've got to be ready to make a *choice* for forgiveness. Yes, forgiveness is a conscious choice, but you may need time before you are ready for that decision. Allow yourself the opportunity to get over the shock so that healing can begin. Just make sure you're using the time to heal, not to nurture bitterness and resentment.

Make a Choice for Forgiveness

When I lived in Oregon one of the pastors in my church, Steve Bearden, helped me realize that I always have a choice in life. Here's what he once wrote in our church's newsletter:

> "I have no choice." I often hear these words when
> someone is describing a painful situation in his life.
> Usually, the person sees himself as a helpless victim of evil
> persons or circumstances. In addition, depression, despair,
> and doubt characterize his thought life. Perhaps most
> damaging is a profound sense of powerlessness coloring
> his perspective. May I lovingly remind us that
> the powerless perspective is diametrically opposed to the
> gospel of Jesus Christ? We possess incredible potential
> for choice and change! Why? Because the person who
> spoke the universe into existence offers to live within our
> beings. He has given us the power to choose Him as Lord
> of our entire lives, thus releasing new possibilities,
> perspectives, and power. And most amazing of all, this
> power to choose is available to every person! No
> exceptions! THE CHOICE IS OURS.

When you are ready forgiveness is yours for the choosing. Ultimately, you are responsible for your choice. Do you want devastation or restoration? Choosing not to forgive brings bitterness, resentment, thoughts of revenge, and devastation. Choosing to forgive brings healing, peace of mind, and restoration. As my friend, Stormie Omartian, once said, "God doesn't ask us to be perfect; He simply asks us to take steps of obedience. We are to say, 'I choose to forgive that person.' *Forgiveness doesn't make the other person right, it makes you free.*"[1]

When you are able to forgive you have cut the strings of bondage that kept a dark cloud hanging over you. Forgiveness is the only way to be free. If you've been hurt, you've got a decision to make: do you want to choose forgiveness?

Possibly you were the victim of child abuse. Or, you might have lived with an alcoholic parent or spouse. Or, you might be the victim of molestation or rape. Maybe, like me, you've always felt inadequate no matter how hard you tried. Those kinds of hurts don't disappear. Blaming another person, however, doesn't make the situation any better.

What are your hurts and confusions? The special healing the Holy Spirit works in your life often comes about through the power of forgiveness. Have you made a choice to utilize this power?

Accept Your Responsibility

Once you have chosen to forgive the person who has hurt you, you will need to take certain steps of restoration. The first step is to accept your responsibility in the situation. You may say, "But I was not at fault. I was just a child and my parents abused me." This may be true, but what about your own resentment, anger, or bitterness? What about the hatred you may have harbored? We all need to examine our response to the situation, just as Julie, a young woman who worked for a large corporation did.

From all indications Julie was a valued employee who had been working at her job for over three years. At every annual work review interview with her bosses she was always highly praised and received a pay raise.

She felt secure in her job until one day, out of the blue,

her supervisor, Nancy, told her she was fired. Julie could hardly believe it. The reason she was fired was a mystery until she learned that Nancy had ordered the firing because she was afraid Julie would eventually get the supervisor's job and Nancy would be out of work.

At first Julie was furious with Nancy and wanted to get revenge. She considered going over Nancy's head and taking her complaints to the company bosses, but she knew it would be her word against Nancy's and could be a messy, mud-slinging battle. She chose instead to get on with her life and start looking for a new job.

This was basically a good decision, but Julie still carried resentment and bitterness. She focused all the blame and responsibility for the job loss on Nancy, harboring ill-will and unkind thoughts toward her. When asked, Julie would explain her job loss this way: "It was all my supervisor's fault. She was jealous of how much attention I received. She just wanted to get rid of me even though I didn't deserve it."

A few weeks later, Julie found a new, comparable job at another company, but this wasn't the end of her bitter feelings toward Nancy. Julie just couldn't forgive what she believed was a terrible injustice.

Because Julie was a Christian, the Lord slowly began to show her that her embittered attitude was wrong. In time she started to look at her situation from a different perspective.

Was she in any way responsible for her firing? After a closer examination Julie was able to admit that there were times when she had purposely tried to make Nancy look bad. She had tried to make herself indispensable to the company and had crossed over the boundaries of her job responsibilities to demonstrate her capability. This infringed on Nancy's territory and caused Nancy to feel threatened.

When Julie was able to see some areas where she was

responsible, she knew she needed to ask Nancy's forgiveness. Although this was a very difficult step to take, she made an appointment to meet Nancy for lunch.

Over lunch Julie apologized to Nancy for the times she had hurt her or inadvertently threatened her job security. As Julie tells it, Nancy's eyes grew wide and filled with tears. She told Julie that she had felt guilty about maneuvering to get Julie fired. She also went on to explain that she had been having problems at home: her son and daughter were both in college, and her husband had recently had a hospital stay. Her financial situation was precarious and she had been afraid that Julie's job performance would cause the company bosses to promote Julie to her position. To prevent this from happening, she'd sent complaints about Julie's work to the bosses along with the notice that she'd had to fire Julie.

Nancy's confession helped Julie to understand Nancy's motivation. They were then able to go their separate ways, each with some measure of peace.

What would have happened if Nancy had not accepted Julie's apology? Would it have meant that Julie should never have apologized in the first place? Of course not! Julie was only responsible before God for her own actions. She was not responsible for Nancy's response.

You must remember that you are only responsible for what God expects from you. You are not responsible for what He expects from someone else. In my relationships with other people it has been so freeing to know that I am not responsible for someone else's actions. I am only responsible before the Lord for my actions. No matter how hard I try, I cannot change anyone else; with God's help, I can only change myself.

When someone has hurt you one of the first questions you may need to ask yourself is: "Have I done anything to cause this?" Before God you need to ask, "Do I need to ask forgiveness of anyone?" The Lord through His Holy Spirit can lead you into the truth. If there is something you have done that needs forgiveness, you'll need to take care of that first.

If after searching your heart before God you have concluded that you did nothing to cause the hurt that has come against you, then the second thing you need to do is ask yourself, "Why has this person hurt me? What do I need to understand?" This line of thought will keep you from feeling rejected and from thinking, "I'm no good. I must deserve this." Instead you'll be able to see that the other person is the one with the problem. Usually when someone hurts you and causes conflicts and problems, there is a hidden agenda. Something else is going on that you may not know about.

At first, when Nancy fired Julie, it seemed to Julie to be a purely mean-spirited and spiteful action. Nancy was cast in the role of the evil villain. However, when Julie had a chance to talk with Nancy she learned about Nancy's terrible financial burdens, plus the added stress of her husband's illness. When Julie began to see what was happening in Nancy's life it was easier to feel compassion for her and to see that although her motivation and her actions were wrong, she had compelling reasons for firing Julie.

Was Nancy truly Julie's enemy? Or was Nancy also a victim? When someone has hurt you it is extremely important that you identify the real enemy.

Identify the Real Enemy

One of the biggest lies that Satan will try and make you believe is that your enemy is a flesh and blood person. He will try and convince you, usually successfully, that another human being is totally responsible for the hurt and pain you are feeling. This is a lie! Your enemy is *never* flesh and blood, *never* another human being. Ephesians 6:12

says, "For we do not wrestle against flesh and blood, but against principalities, against powers, against the rulers of the darkness of this age, against spiritual hosts of wickedness in the heavenly places." The enemy isn't the person who hurt you. The enemy of your soul is Satan and his spiritual forces of evil.

Let me show you what I mean by telling you how Satan influenced Karen. Karen came from a Christian home marked by very strict and rigid discipline. Although her childhood was basically normal and secure, things changed when Karen reached her teen years.

When she was sixteen years old Karen's parents began having marital difficulties. Karen's father eventually moved to another city, while her mother, Jeanne, tried to hold the family together. Due to the drastic change in her family structure, Karen was confused and unhappy. Angry at her father for leaving them, she lashed out at Jeanne, refusing to obey her mother's authority. When Karen was punished for this she and Jeanne became embroiled in loud, accusatory, and counterproductive arguments.

Soon Karen began to rebel in earnest. She started hanging out with the wrong crowd, staying out until all hours of the morning, never bothering to let her mother know where she was or what she was doing. Karen's defiance escalated, and Jeanne, trying to deal with her own marriage problems while raising Karen and two younger siblings, was unable to cope with Karen's rebellion. The arguments continued, and finally, one night after a bitter row, Jeanne asked Karen to leave. At the time Karen was happy to oblige. That night she slept over at a friend's house.

The next day when Karen went back to her home she found that all the locks had been changed and her belongings were packed and waiting for her on the front porch. Karen couldn't believe it. She wasn't too worried though; she was sure her mother would soon relent. In the meantime she asked to stay at her friend's house a few more nights.

Weeks went by, and although distraught by the situation, both Jeanne and Karen were unable to come to an understanding. Karen wanted to live at home and do as she pleased. Jeanne would not agree to this and still refused to let Karen back into the house. In fact, when Karen was no longer able to stay at her friend's house, Jeanne signed the papers allowing Karen to be placed in a foster home. In Jeanne's mind there was no alternative. Karen's problems were more than she could handle at the time.

For the next two years Karen lived in several different foster homes. During that time she didn't see her family. Even though she heard through the grapevine that her parents were reconciled, they did not call and ask Karen to move back home. By this time she was a very hardened, angry young adult, and she focused all her rage and resentment on her mother. Although her father was far from perfect, he had been gone during all the turmoil. In Karen's mind Jeanne was to blame for all of the problems.

Over the next seventeen years Karen experienced many ups and downs, but she worked hard to make something of her life. She got a job, eventually got married, and had two children. During those years, however, she never tried to contact her family. Although she thought about them often, she was still too angry with Jeanne to ever make the first move. Karen just could not forgive her mother for kicking her out of the house.

Many people, when faced with a similar sense of betrayal or injustice, cut the offending person(s) out of their life forever. They carry a lifetime grudge and refuse to be free of their pain. This is what happened to Karen for seventeen years, and could have continued for a lifetime, except for one important fact. Three years ago, Karen became a Christian.

When Karen became a Christian she realized that her

bitterness toward her mother was wrong. She knew she needed to forgive Jeanne for what had happened so many years ago. Through studying God's Word and spending time in counseling with her pastor, Karen learned one of the most crucial elements of forgiveness: she learned to identify her real enemy.

Karen learned that her enemy was not Jeanne; her enemy was Satan. Jeanne, along with Karen's father and Karen herself, had been used by Satan to break up Karen's home life, but Satan was the true culprit for all of the destruction. Satan, not Jeanne, wanted to destroy Karen. Instead of hating her mother, Karen learned to see her as a human being who made the mistake of listening to Satan's plan for destruction. By nursing hatred and bitterness toward Jeanne, Karen had encouraged her own destruction—just what Satan wanted.

Once Karen could stop blaming Jeanne as the person responsible for hurting her, she began to see her mother in a more compassionate light. Since Karen was now a mother herself, she could better understand Jeanne's point of view. For the first time she began to wonder if Jeanne had also suffered pain because of the rift between them.

When Karen realized that her true enemy was Satan she was able to release her feelings of bitterness toward Jeanne. The very next month she decided to contact her family and let them know she was still alive. She'd always known how to reach them since they still lived in her old hometown. Living in a city just two hours away, Karen asked her parents to come to her home for a reunion.

The very next day Karen's parents were on her doorstep. As they all embraced amid many tears, Karen heard her mother say "I'm sorry" for the first time. Later that afternoon Jeanne shared with Karen about the heartbreak she'd felt for the last seventeen years. Karen learned that after her parents were reconciled, they had still had many problems to resolve. Since Karen was a "wild" teenager at the time, Jeanne was afraid her presence in the home would cause further disruption, making it impossible for her marriage to work out. With Karen's two younger siblings still at home, Jeanne was also afraid that Karen would influence them to rebel. Although she now regrets it, at the time Jeanne felt she was making the right decision. As the years passed and she didn't hear from Karen, she was afraid to try and find her. Jeanne feared that if she contacted Karen, the arguments would begin again, and more pain would be inflicted by stirring up old wounds.

As Karen and Jeanne were able to listen, communicate, and forgive each other, they each learned what the past seventeen years had been like for the other. They also realized that neither one of them had wanted the estrangement. Only Satan delighted in the estrangement that had caused so much pain. He was the real enemy in both of their lives.

There will be times when, just like Jeanne and Karen, you'll either be hurt or hurt someone else. As human beings we are fallible. Yes, another human being can bring great misery into your life, but the real problem begins when you mistakenly identify that person as your enemy.

You've probably seen it many times: the newly married couple who are always holding hands and gazing into each other's eyes. When they sit down together they only need eight inches of space on an eight-foot couch! They crowd into one another to be as closely attached as possible; after all, they are in love!

But what happens many times through the ensuing months and years? Sadly, the huge couch begins to seem much too small. They don't even want to be in the same room together. They can each recite a long list of all the things they don't like about the other person and they feel they are no longer in love.

Do you know what has happened to that couple? Satan has caused them to believe that their own mate is the enemy when all along it has been Satan coming against the union in their home. The devil himself is seeking to devour and destroy their home, but he's got them believing that they are at odds with one another.

Not only in marriages, this division often appears between parent and child, brother and sister, friend and friend. If you've ever raised a teenager you know what I mean. Suddenly the greatest enemy you have seems to be your teenager. Or, vice versa—your child may feel that his greatest enemy is his mother or father. In this situation no one gets along, and constant bickering or all-out fights characterize the home. Satan has you believing a family member is the enemy, when in reality he is using the strife to destroy your home.

If you're starting over, like me, you know what it's like to get pulled up by the roots and transplanted somewhere else. Pain, revenge, hatred, resentment, and bitterness blind you to the fact that your real enemy is *not* flesh and blood. The enemy against your soul is Satan. He is the one who seeks to destroy you, but as long as he can keep you thinking another human being is the enemy, he's winning the battle.

How can you turn the tables on him? By *refusing* to concentrate on the human being that he used to hurt you. Instead of seeing your betrayer as someone who did something *to you,* you start to see that person as someone who had something *done to him.*

To understand this you've got to realize that Satan is the prince of this earthly world and right now we're living in his kingdom. Yes, through Jesus Christ we have a new kingdom established within us, but our outer world is ruled by Satan. As long as we live in his kingdom, we are going to come against him; however, we don't need to be held captive. When anyone acts in an evil way against us we must realize that *he* is captive to Satan's kingdom. Somewhere along the line, even if that person is a Christian, he has allowed an evil force into his life.

When a person commits an immoral act, for instance, that is not something that occurs on the spur of the moment. Little by little the trap is laid in a person's thoughts. Once a person crosses his conscience line a few times, once he has violated some of his standards, greater violations occur.

Satan's evil force is always pricking at you, always attacking you. Until Satan gets you he is always scheming to get you. How can you or anyone war against Satan? Ephesians 6:11 says, "Put on the whole armor of God, that you may be able to stand against the wiles of the devil."

After you put on the full armor of God, you've got to know the location of the battlefield. Just as no other flesh and blood person is your enemy, you can't fight this battle in the flesh. We're engaged in a spiritual warfare that must be fought on the battlefield of prayer.

Prayer Is the Battleground

We have been taught all of our lives to live by our senses. We are told that what we can see, hear, taste, touch, and smell is the real world. In contrast to this the Scriptures tell us that what we know and experience through our senses is one day going to vanish in an instant. We are not now living in a real world; the *real* world is the one that is going to last forever—the spirit world.

When you can see the pain and the hurt of this earthly world as a spiritual problem, you then realize you must do battle in the spirit through prayer. Once you deal with your problems through prayer you've brought the enemy into God's kingdom, and Satan is going to lose.

The book of Daniel, chapter 10, gives an example of this spiritual battle. Daniel had been concerned for some time about his people who seemed to fall prey to every evil scheme, every false doctrine the enemy planned. Daniel saw ruin ahead, so he went to God in prayer for his nation.

Now he didn't just go and say, "God, I've come here for a

few moments this morning, and I just want you to know that my nation is in trouble. Please help them out. See you tomorrow."

Instead, the Bible says that he prayed and fasted for twenty-one days. He abstained from all the rituals of the flesh so that he might understand the way of the spirit. At the end of the twenty-one days Daniel received a vision from God. God's messenger said to Daniel:

> Don't be frightened, Daniel, for your request has been heard in heaven and was answered the very first day you began to fast before the Lord and pray for understanding; that very day I was sent here to meet you. But for twenty-one days the mighty Evil Spirit who overrules the kingdom of Persia blocked my way. Then Michael, one of the top officers of the heavenly army, came to help me, so that I was able to break through these spirit rulers of Persia. (Dan. 10:12–13, Living Bible)

Here's the picture: A man on earth is facing a problem in his life. He identifies the spiritual battle and his real enemy and goes to prayer. He spends time in prayer and utters his request to the Almighty Father. The very first day he makes the request the Father hears it and dispatches the answer. In between God's answer and man's request are evil forces resisting the coming of God's answer. For twenty-one days Daniel stayed on the battlefield of prayer, and finally the answer came.

The all-powerful God could choose to just break through the resistance and bring the answer immediately. However, God wants us to continue in the battle so that we can become spiritually equipped. We, as Christians, are Christ's bride, and His bride has to get ready. She has to be prepared so that one day she can do royal duty with Christ in eternity. The place where the bride gets ready is prayer.

Barbara Johnson, a wonderful Christian woman, is the author of the book, *Where Does a Mother Go to Resign?*[2] In this book she shares the heartbreak and pain she endured when she learned that her adult son was a homosexual. She had already lost two grown sons in death and her third son's homosexuality came as a final, crushing blow. When she first discovered her son's homosexuality, he was still living at home. However, within one week of her discovery he had moved out without a word. He had been a strong Christian young man who was a leader in the church youth group, so his secret life-style was especially devastating. When he moved out he told no one where he was going, and she wasn't able to see or talk with him again for a year.

According to Barbara, losing her son to homosexuality was worse in many ways than losing her other sons in death. At least she had the comfort of knowing her other sons were in heaven with Christ. Not being able to know if her homosexual son was alive or dead, and knowing he was caught in Satan's web of lies and deceit, was almost unendurable.

Barbara had to literally pick up the pieces of her shattered family (she still had a husband and one teenage son left at home), and try to go on with her life. Anyone who has suffered the loss of a loved one, no matter what the cause, knows what it is like to have to start over again. Most days you feel as if an arm or a leg were missing. You just can't function in the same way and you often expect the missing person to be there. You learn to take things daily, minute by minute as the healing process begins.

Barbara was in counseling, prayer, and agony over her homosexual son for one year before she was even able to see him again. Sadly, seeing him again did not bring about a miracle in his life. She had to learn to rebuild her world to include a homosexual son. But she never stopped praying. She stayed on the battlefield of prayer for eleven years— the only place where she could stand a chance of winning against Satan's evil hold over her son. Sometimes I'm sure it must have seemed hopeless. Sometimes I'm sure she wanted to quit, but she believed in the power of prayer and kept fighting.

Finally, after eleven years of praying, her son was delivered from the homosexual life-style and came to her to ask for forgiveness. What a victorious day!

You see, there is a real enemy and a real battlefield and there are real victories to be won! Yes, the battle may be long, it could last for years. But the only chance you have of winning the battle for yourself or for someone else is to stay on the battlefield.[3]

I would encourage you to explore this area. Learning how to pray will change your life dramatically for the better! Rather than plotting revenge against the human being who hurt you, prayer will enable you to practice compassion.

Give Up Revenge—Practice Compassion

Pastor Claude Robold had a great crisis experience in his own church ministry, and during this time his father (also a minister) would say to him, "Have you suffered to the shedding of blood?"

Claude would say, "No."

And his dad would say, "Then you're okay."

Christ suffered to the shedding of blood for our sake; for our sin. Nobody has done anything to me like what my sin did to Christ. Nobody has done anything to you like what your sin did to Christ. Thinking about that changes your perspective, doesn't it? Psalm 103 has been so helpful to me when I consider this new perspective on forgiveness.

> The LORD is merciful and gracious,
> Slow to anger, and abounding in mercy.
> He will not always strive with us,
> Nor will He keep His anger forever.

> He has not dealt with us according to our sins,
> Nor punished us according to our iniquities.
> For as the heavens are high above the earth,
> So great is His mercy toward those who fear Him;
> As far as the east is from the west,
> So far has He removed our transgressions from us.
> (vv. 8–12)

Since these verses are true then you and I have not been treated as our sin deserves. If God has done this for you, you need to pass it along to your fellowman. No matter who wounds you, God still loves you and you don't have to live your life in the pit of pain and despair. You were not worthy of His love, but He thought you worthy and has made you worthy through Christ Jesus. You need to be in a position to be able to extend this same love to others. Staying in anger or hatred keeps you bound to the problem. If you and I are truly honest with ourselves, we know that we have no right to sit in judgment on someone else. Only God has that right and He has chosen instead to extend mercy. How can we choose otherwise?

For instance, I had a woman completely lie about me. Following my divorce, after I'd moved to another city, she told people I'd once had an affair with her ex-husband. This was a total untruth! I couldn't believe it when a mutual friend told me what this woman had been saying. The pain of my divorce was horrible enough without an old friend making up lies about me. My first thought was, *I don't deserve this!* And then I started to wonder about her hidden motivations. What had caused this woman to deliberately lie about me? I knew it was out of character for her. What had happened to bring this kind of spiritual darkness on her?

I had a choice to make. I could choose to get angry, start loudly proclaiming my innocence, and tell the whole world (or as much of it as possible) what a liar she turned out to be. Or, I could choose to try to understand and forgive her. If I had gotten angry and told everyone that she was a liar, what good would it have done her or me? Her sin was not my struggle; my struggle was with the enemy of my soul and her soul. I needed to war against Satan for myself, and for her, when she couldn't war for herself. To do this, I had to be on the battlefield of prayer, not plotting my revenge against her.

I was in prayer about this situation for quite some time, dealing with my anger toward this woman. At the time my Bible study group was studying Ephesians. One day during my daily devotions I read Ephesians 4:31–32 which says, "Let all bitterness, wrath, anger, clamor, and evil speaking be put away from you, with all malice. And be kind to one another, tenderhearted, forgiving one another, just as God in Christ also forgave you." From that point on, whenever I felt the anger rising I would think of that verse and make a choice for forgiveness. Later, I learned that this woman had been having extreme difficulties at that point in her life. These stresses caused her to lash out at me, and I'm sure at others as well.

If someone lies about you, you may need to confront the person. In my case I couldn't confront the woman face-to-face because I didn't want to betray the confidence of the friend who informed me about the lie. Instead, I asked the friend to go to this woman and tell her I knew what she'd said. In my situation this took care of the problem. If it hadn't, I would then have confronted the woman myself, in a spirit of reconciliation.

When someone hurts you you naturally feel angry and offended. Releasing some of your anger in appropriate ways can be liberating, but holding a grudge keeps you wounded, with no chance for true healing. I once knew of a woman whose fiancé had jilted her at the altar. She started dating and sleeping with many different men, all the while thinking, *This will show him that I'm desirable!*

Instead she just ended up seriously hurting herself. She threw her self-respect away in an attempt to get revenge.

Holding a grudge or plotting revenge are subtle forms of suicide—they do *you* much more harm than they do someone else. Letting go, however, can be very difficult.

Forgiving Again . . . and Again

During the time immediately following my divorce I had many emotional upheavals and a huge period of adjustment. I was living alone in a great big house and was very lonely. The Lord provided my twin sister, Judy, and her husband who had just returned from the mission field in Guam and needed a place to live temporarily. Their coming to live with me was a true answer to prayer. Not only did I have my twin sister for company, but also a friend, counselor, and pastor in my brother-in-law, Dick.

After they moved in I seemed to be more stable emotionally. I was in better control of my anger and thought that I was really recovering until I found out that my former husband, who had moved to another state, was coming to town for two days. Since I had just returned from a trip to Europe to visit our son, Bobby, I assumed that my ex-husband would be calling me to find out how Bobby was doing. In hindsight I can see that I shouldn't have jumped to that conclusion. I stayed home all that day waiting for his call. Although a part of me didn't want him to call, a part of me hoped that he would. When he didn't call that day I felt both relief and anger. I was a bundle of contradicting emotions.

The second day, irrationally, I again waited all day and there was still no call. By then I was very upset and crying. That evening my brother-in-law, Dick, said to me, "Joanne, you can't take this to bed with you. You must deal with this *now*. If you don't it will deepen and you will really be in trouble."

Through my tears and pain I heard him continue, "You must do something to get this hurt and anger out or you will become physically ill. I want you to go outside and yell as loudly as you can. Just yell and let it all out. Get rid of some of the junk inside you."

Fortunately for me I lived in the country at that time and so I didn't have to worry about the neighbors. I decided to take his advice and went outside. At that point I began to talk *very loudly* to God. I couldn't quite bring myself to yell, but I was able to cry out before God about the pain that I felt inside. Of course it wasn't news to God; He'd known all along how I was feeling, but I did begin to feel better.

After a while I was physically drained and decided to go back in the house. Once inside I asked Dick, "Okay, now what do I do? I feel better and some of the pressure is gone. What's next?"

Very gently Dick said, "What do you think you should do?" Realizing that I was talking to a pastor and wanting to sound "spiritual," I said, "Now we should pray."

With love Dick paused for a moment and then said, "That can come later. Think, Joanne . . . what do you need to do now?"

As Dick spoke, new tears began to flow, only this time they were not tears of anger, but of peace. The Holy Spirit whispered the knowledge into my heart and I knew what I had to do. "Oh, yes," I said, "I need to forgive all over again."

Matthew 18:21–22 says, "Then Peter came to Him and said, 'Lord, how often shall my brother sin against me, and I forgive him? Up to seven times?' Jesus said to him, 'I do not say to you, up to seven times, but up to seventy times seven.' " For me, seventy times seven can sometimes be all in *one* day! Forgiveness and healing often need to come again and again.

If You Forgive, Will You Forget?

I'm often asked, "If you forgive, will you forget?" and I've found in my own experience that the answer is sometimes yes and sometimes no. If the hurt was minor, you may also forget. If, on the other hand, you experienced a deep and major hurt, forgiveness will not also bring forgetfulness. There may always be times when you will remember the hurt, but after you've experienced forgiveness the memory will not evoke feelings of bitterness and resentment. You may sometimes feel sad or even have flashes of anger, but you will not linger on those feelings.

In my own life I've discovered that the healing power of forgiveness is evident when I am able to wish the offending person well. This doesn't mean that you will welcome the person back into your life with open arms; you may still go separate ways, but at least you can pray for God's best in his or her life.

As this wonderful paraphrase of Romans 8:28 states: "The Lord may not have planned that this should overtake me, but He has most certainly permitted it. Therefore, though it were an attack of an enemy, by the time it reaches me, it has the Lord's permission and therefore all is well. He will make it work together with all life's experiences for good" (Navigators).

Through the power of forgiveness you too can know the joy of seeing all life's experiences work for good. As tough as it may be, forgiveness is the only way to free yourself from pain and resentment.

SELF-WORTH:
Understanding Your Priceless Value

*What lies behind us
and what lies before us
are tiny matters compared to
what lies within us.*

—William Morrow[1]

CHAPTER FIVE

In 1964 I was a young mother with two small children. I was employed at a local cannery on a long assembly line, working the night shift so that I could be with my preschool children during the day while my husband was home with them at night. Back then I usually wore a white work uniform, little or no makeup, and an ugly hair net. When I look at photographs taken during that time I can scarcely believe it's me. My self-concept was at an all-time low and the photographs document it. No one would have thought that within three years I would be modeling professionally and teaching a self-improvement course. Nor would they have thought that within four years I'd be crowned Mrs. Oregon 1968, and would compete in the Mrs. America pageant. In fact, in 1964 even I wouldn't have thought it possible, but that's exactly what happened.

How did I go from being an unattractive cannery worker to being a self-improvement teacher, pageant winner, and model? It started when I learned about my true self-worth and began to realize my own God-given, unique talents. In short, I built a positive self-concept.

Since that time, many years ago, I've been teaching and speaking on the subject of developing a positive self-concept—the one subject I never tire of sharing with others. Building a positive self-concept is the key to unlocking so many of the problems that face us.

There are three basic terms that I use when talking about self-concept:

- Self-worth—how God sees you

- Self-image—how you see yourself

- Self-esteem—how you feel about yourself

You can see by the list how closely related they are to each other. To build your self-concept, you've got to have a healthy, developed sense of your self-worth, self-image, and self-esteem. Your self-image and self-esteem are two sides of the same coin. Your self-worth, however, is the foundation for your self-image and self-esteem, and the starting place for building a positive self-concept.

Self-worth: How God Sees You

When I was in high school a girl in my class, Ellen, was taking a professional modeling course. I remember wishing at the time that I could join her in those classes. Since Ellen was doing it and everyone said I was prettier than she, I thought maybe I'd have a chance. It all sounded so glamorous and exciting, just what I needed to fulfill my daydreams about being Elizabeth Taylor! Yes, a modeling career sounded wonderful but was absolutely forbidden since I was a Christian. At the time my parents didn't even allow me to wear lipstick. So instead of modeling I went to college, got married, had two children, and then started working in a cannery to make ends meet. Not exactly Elizabeth Taylor, but at the time I didn't believe that my dreams could come true anyway.

While working at the local cannery, I met another worker named Jill. Since we both worked the night shift on the same monotonous assembly line, we began talking to each other. Our personalities clicked immediately, and we have now been friends for almost thirty years. Jill was having a problem with her self-esteem and wanted to take a self-improvement course offered by a local modeling agency. She was shy and uncomfortable about going to the first class by herself, so she asked me to go along with her for moral support. Of course, I was dying to go, but I let Jill think that she was convincing me to join her! That way I'd be able to salvage my pride if the agency rejected me.

The night of the first introductory class stands out vividly in my memory. The agency's owner and the other instructors were so friendly and encouraging. They thought I'd be a wonderful model. I could hardly believe it! Of course, I know they were doing a good sales job, but at the time their encouragement meant all the world to me. That night Jill and I signed up for the course.

The self-improvement classes taught me to believe in myself. The agency's owner and director, Sue, made a point of praising the progress I was making. When the self-improvement classes were over I enrolled in the modeling course. My dreams were becoming reality. Through the agency I started getting professional modeling jobs. My confidence grew and I began to see new possibilities for my life.

When the modeling course ended the agency had an annual graduation ceremony with awards and prizes. That year I won the Miss Congeniality award from the other students and also took top honors as Model of the Year. Part of the competition for being chosen Model of the Year included giving a speech. Even though my major in college was speech, I'd never given a speech outside of the classroom. This time my audience included prominent people from my community. I was scared to death, but after giving my speech, the audience response was tremendous. People I didn't know came up to me and said things like, "charming smile," and "such good rapport with an audience." God was showing me a new direction for my life, and I was definitely on cloud nine.

To my further surprise, Sue, the agency's owner, called me into her office and asked me if I'd like to be the director of a new modeling school she was opening. I was amazed! Here was a new career opportunity being handed to me! I didn't have to keep working at the cannery. I could actually realize my dream!

Sue was the first person who taught me to believe in myself. She saw the potential that God had given me and she gave me the opportunity to develop that potential. As the director and instructor of a self-improvement and modeling agency, I was able to use my God-given talents in a much more effective way than I could working at a cannery. Through Sue's encouragement I started to see that God had a special plan for my life—a plan that only I could fulfill and that required that I believe in myself.

I needed someone to help me realize that God placed great value on my life. Possibly you need to realize the same thing. In God's eyes you *are* priceless. You were made in His image. He created you and has great plans for you. *There is a plan for you that nobody else can fulfill.* That's how special, unique, and wonderful you are in God's sight. You must realize how wonderful God thinks you are, not so that you can shout it to the world, but so that you can give glory to Him by fulfilling His plan for your life.

Do you know that God proclaimed your innate worth when He loved you enough to send Jesus to die for you? Romans 5:6–8 says, "For when we were still without strength, in due time Christ died for the ungodly. For scarcely for a righteous man will one die; yet perhaps for a good man someone would even dare to die. But God demonstrates His own love toward us, in that while we were still sinners, Christ died for us."

Basing your self-worth on anything other than God's declaration of your innate worth will always lead to disappointment. Through the years people have tried to find their self-worth in their jobs or personal relationships. They believe that if only a certain person cared for them or if they could land such and such a job, then they'd be fulfilled. Temporarily, these sorts of things may help, but what happens when the job or relationship fails? When I realized a dream by becoming the director of a modeling agency, I still couldn't base my self-worth on that job, or else ultimately I'd be disappointed. A job or relationship, no matter how perfect, can still fail you. Your self-worth must not depend on circumstances. Through God's work in my heart and life, I realized that He was the originator of my self-worth—I'm valuable because He says I am. This is true for you as well—you're valuable because He says you are.

I also believe that God says to each one of us, "It makes Me very sad when you don't realize how much I love you and that you were made in My image." Do you hear Him saying that to you today? It's never too late to discover all that God has in store for you. It doesn't matter if you're over forty, fifty, or ninety! If you can say, "I want to learn new things. I want to dream some new dreams," it's not too late.

God loves you just as you are, no matter what you may have done with your life. If you were the only person on the earth, He would still have sent Jesus to die for you. Too many people don't understand this great love and acceptance. One woman who attended my seminar wrote to me: "I'm nothing. I've lived all my life needing to be something and someone. I've never done things right, I've just survived and existed—and poorly at that. I've always had the desire and terrible need to be someone! Even with God, I'm at the bottom of the ladder and have so far to go."

What terrible pain and suffering this dear woman has endured to write such a heart-rending note! Somewhere along the line she has come to believe all the wrong things about herself. The truth is that she already is someone of great worth and she's definitely not at the bottom of God's ladder—He doesn't have one! When we accept Jesus as our Savior we become heirs of God, brothers and sisters. We are a family—not a corporate ladder—and everyone is equal.

Yes, it's true that in God's eyes our righteousness is as filthy rags.[2] But our worth as a person is still priceless. We may not be perfect, but God doesn't expect us to be. He only desires that we allow Christ's perfection to be evident in our lives.

You don't have to perform to please God. He has created you and He is already pleased with His creation. Although He does not like the wrongs you have committed, He loves *you*. This knowledge can change your life, just as it did for a friend of mine, Anne.

Anne's Uniqueness to God

I first met Anne when I traveled to her home state for a seminar. I found myself drawn to this timid, but beautiful woman and wondered what had caused her to doubt her abilities. We spoke after the evening session, and she shared some of her background with me.

Anne was married to an alcoholic. She and her husband, John, had been high school sweethearts and had grown up together. When they were married John professed Christianity and Anne looked forward to a long and happy marriage. In Anne's case, after twenty years of marriage, only the "long" part had come true.

Both Anne and John had a problem with low self-esteem. John worked for a demanding corporation and he thrived when business was going well. But he drowned himself in alcohol when problems arose. After a while the alcohol took over, and he no longer needed the excuse of a failed business opportunity to trigger the drinking.

Anne hated seeing John drinking, but since her own father had also been an alcoholic, she knew just how to facilitate John's problem. Anne became John's doormat. She thought that if she surrendered control of her life to John he would be more interested in her and feel a special bond. In fact, she found out that the opposite was true. After she surrendered control he was not nearly as interested in her. The very thing she craved she missed getting. John began a series of extramarital affairs, staying out most nights either drinking or womanizing. When he was home he verbally abused Anne, telling her in many different ways that she was worthless.

Anne made John's life easier by making excuses for him. She lied to cover his absences from work, defended him to her friends, and constantly walked around on egg shells. She lived in fear of doing something that would aggravate his drinking. In many ways she blamed herself for his problem. In her mind she said, "If only I were a better wife. If only I were more submissive to my husband he would eventually come back to the Lord." She read all the books on "how to be the wife of a happy husband" and was taught that if she were an obedient, wonderful wife, she would be able to turn John into a wonderful husband. Therefore, since her husband verbally abused her, cheated on her, and was an alcoholic—far from wonderful—she believed it was her fault. Caught in a destructive, abusive relationship, she had started to believe death was the only answer. I urged Anne to talk with her pastor or a professional Christian counselor, and I promised to keep in touch with her.

Years later Anne shared with me that my seminar had been a turning point in her life. For the first time she began to see hope for her battered self-esteem. She began to really learn about God's unconditional love for her and His estimation of her worth.

Anne had always put a lot of pressure on herself to perform. She thought that being a "perfect" wife and mother would solve her problems. Recently, she said to me, "I was always trying so hard to be a good mother and wife, and nothing seemed to work. God had to reach me at my lowest point and say, 'It's okay. I love you whether you get up out of bed ever again or not. You can stay in bed with the covers over your head all day and I'll still love you.' When I finally realized that God loved me forever, no matter what I did or didn't do, it brought such freedom."

Anne realized what we all need to realize: that God places great value on us and loves us just as we are. Since this is true, we can assume He doesn't want us to spend our lives feeling worthless. He desires that we understand and appreciate our value so that He can use us for His glory.

During my crisis experience I sometimes wondered if God's love for me would change because of the divorce. I sometimes listened to Satan's lie that God wouldn't love me anymore. I'm so thankful that God was always near me to help dispel the lie. He constantly assured me through prayer and His word that He loved me and always would. Like many people before me, I've come through my crisis experience with the unshakeable belief that God loves me. Sometimes I wondered where He was, but I always knew He loved me!

What's keeping you from fully understanding God's love and wonderful plan for your life? Are you involved in an abusive relationship? If you are, your self-esteem is constantly being brutalized. You may never build your self-esteem while staying in the abusive situation.

Anne's Reconciliation and Restoration

In some cases, the only way to bring about change is to leave the abusive situation so that restoration can begin. That's what Anne decided to do after counseling sessions with her pastor. With his help she came to a very painful, but necessary decision. Since John was still drinking heavily, womanizing, and verbally abusing her, this constantly tore down what little self-esteem she was building and destroyed any chance she had to be a witness for the Lord. Her pastor helped her to see that a period of separation from John, motivated by love, was the only answer so that restoration and reconciliation could begin.

For most situations in life, when dealing with normal people, going the extra mile or turning the other cheek will work. But with people addicted to alcohol, drugs, gambling—any kind of addiction—you can't deal with them in a normal way. If you go the extra mile, they take advantage of it and it feeds their addiction. You end up supporting the problem.

In Anne's case she loved John very much. She wanted to have a whole and healthy marriage, but she'd given too much—she'd given away her personhood. When she decided to separate from John for a time, her desire was for reconciliation. Instead of saying, "My marriage is on the rocks and I'm being devastated as a person, therefore I have to run," Anne was able to say, "Not only is my life being devastated, but John's life as well. I've got to get out of this situation so we can get the proper insight on how to bring about restoration so that reconciliation is possible."

I want to make one thing perfectly clear: Anne did *not* leave with divorce in mind. Divorce is usually motivated by devastation. Instead, she removed herself from the abusive situation with *restoration* as her motive.

Restoration in broken, abusive relationships often cannot come unless there is a period of separation. Many people who hit rock bottom flee the abusive situation with no thought for reconciliation. As far as they are concerned the relationship is only fit for destruction. In God's sight, however, the chance for restoration is always there, as long as both people want it.

The truth of the matter is that people with a chemical dependency will not change unless they think they might lose something. They often need a separation to convince them they require help to change the situation.

Anne had been supporting John's problem all along. Finally, she had to be able to say to him, "Taking care of you has made me feel worthless and has also helped you to destroy yourself. I cannot take care of you anymore, even though I want to so badly it breaks my heart." Anne had to make a choice for wholeness in her life. She had to make room to allow God to work.

While this may not happen in every situation, when Anne decided to remove herself and her children from the abusive situation, things changed dramatically. Her children began doing better in school and their whole outlook and attitude improved. Instead of staying in a relationship which brought no glory to God, robbed her of healthy self-esteem, and left her children feeling insecure from all the havoc, Anne took some responsibility for her own life.

During her separation from John, Anne began attending a women's Bible study. The women there were encouraging and loving, just what Anne needed. Anne soon discovered that she loved studying God's Word and easily memorized Scripture. When the other women in her group helped her discover her God-given intelligence, they encouraged Anne to go back to college where she pursued a degree in counseling.

You too can experience restoration in your life. How? By seeing yourself as God sees you. As you begin to realize all the potential you have and all the exciting things God has planned for you, your life can be made new.

Self-image: How You See Yourself

The choice is yours: if you want to change your self-image, you've got to start by believing what God says about you. What will you decide? Are you going to continue to believe Satan's lies that you're worthless? Or are you going to believe God when He says that through Jesus you are a king and priest to Him. (See Rev. 1:6) You are a child of God, born of a royal line!

In 1964, as an unattractive cannery worker, I sometimes had trouble imagining that I was really God's royal child. When I looked in the mirror after long, hard hours working the night shift, I certainly didn't feel very royal. In fact, I sometimes wondered how God could love me at all.

Not until I started reading and studying Psalm 139 did I discover God's intimate knowledge of me and His matchless love. Through this psalm I developed a special exercise that helped to raise my low self-esteem. Try the following steps.

1. Read Psalm 139:1–18 and jot down all the points that stand out to you. Next, list all the things recorded in this psalm that God knows about you. Do you see that God knows everything about you, even more than you know about yourself?

2. Now read Romans 8:38–39. Let the message sink into your consciousness. Not only does God know everything about you, but nothing can separate you from His love. If He loves you even after knowing you better than you know yourself, who are you to disagree?

3. Take time to reflect on God's love for you and His intimate knowledge of you. Thank Him for what a unique person you are.

4. Read Romans 11:29 and Romans 12:4–8. *Everyone* is gifted. You are good at something—I guarantee it! Do you know what it is? Whatever it is, God has called you to do it. If you don't know, commit yourself to finding out. Ask God to reveal to you your special talents and gifts. God's blueprint for your life is written in your talents and abilities. One of the most important things to remember is that your gift, plus diligence, will equal satisfaction in life. Begin today to fulfill God's plan for you. Let Philippians 4:13, "I can do all things through Christ who strengthens me," be your motto.

5. Repeat this exercise as often as necessary!

As you begin to renew your mind, which is a continuous process, I would highly recommend that you spend at least one hour every day in prayer and reading God's Word. David Seamands, in his excellent book, *Healing For Damaged Emotions*,[3] suggests praying this beautiful prayer on a daily basis: "Lord . . . I am going to listen to your opinion of me, and let you reprogram me until your loving estimate of me becomes a part of my life . . . right down to my innermost feelings." This prayer is an effective weapon in erasing the negative tapes that Satan wants you to play in your mind—the tapes that tell you you're worthless, a nobody, a nothing; the negative tapes that may have started playing the day you were born.

Changing the Negative Tapes

After my daughter, Deanna, gave birth to my first grandson, Aron, she was recuperating in a hospital room with another new mother. That day, as Deanna lay in her partitioned area of the room, she was shocked to hear the other mother calling her newborn baby every obscenity in the book. Some of the nicer names were "ugly face" and "butt head." The rest of the names are totally unprintable. Deanna couldn't believe her ears. Only a one-in-a million mother would do such a thing.

Nine years and four adopted children later, Deanna gave birth again to my granddaughter, Fallon. Once again she was in a hospital room with another new mother and unbelievably, this new mother also began calling her tiny baby every obscene name imaginable. Deanna lay there listening to the raw and ugly words and silently wept. If an innocent newborn baby was already hearing such hateful words, what would be in store for that child in the years to come? Obviously the problem of negative tapes being started at birth did not happen only one time in a million.

Maybe your negative tapes play raw and ugly words that have been aimed at you since birth. Maybe you hear those negative tapes playing in your mind every hour of every day. The hurt and pain may run so deep you don't even know you're hearing them; you may think it's the truth about yourself.

When I was a little girl I had blond, naturally curly hair, and people were always quoting an infamous little poem to me that went like this:

> There once was a girl
> Who had a little curl
> Right in the middle of her forehead.
> And when she was good,
> She was very, very good,
> But when she was bad—
> She was *horrid.*

I know that the people who said this to me meant no harm, but unfortunately, they didn't emphasize the *very good* part, they emphasized the *horrid.* Soon I started thinking of myself as quite horrid, especially when it seemed to me that I got into more trouble than my quiet and shy twin sister.

Not only did I constantly hear that negative little poem during my growing-up years, but when I became a mother I started saying it to my own blond, curly-haired daughter. It seemed that there was no end to the damaging cycle of that particular poem. I had to learn how to escape from my own negative tapes by the renewing of my mind.

If you're struggling with negative tapes that seem to have no end, my heart weeps with you. My prayer is that you'll be able to change those tapes through the power of God when you decide to believe all the positive things that God has to say about you. Spend as much time as possible in prayer and reading His Word. Unfortunately, even one negative tape can spoil a whole series of positive ones.

To illustrate this, I often tell a fictitious story about

Deanna baking me a birthday cake. In this story she gathers up all the finest ingredients and blends them all together until she has made a perfect batter. Then, just before she puts the cake into the oven, she sprinkles just a spoonful of sand into the mixture. The cake comes out of the oven looking and smelling heavenly. When it cools she ices it with my favorite chocolate frosting and decorates it with beautiful yellow roses.

That night I arrive at her home for my birthday celebration. When I see the cake I can hardly wait to take a bite. She puts a huge piece on the plate in front of me and I dig into it with gusto. The first bite tastes absolutely delicious until I suddenly feel sand gritting between my teeth. As I reach for a glass of water to rinse my mouth, I decide to try just one more bite. Maybe there was something on my fork, I reason. Surely there couldn't be sand in the cake.

The second bite is just as bad as the first, and my face cannot hide the displeasure I feel at crunching on sand. I look at Deanna and say, "Honey, was that ever a delicious cake—except for one thing—why in the world did you put sand in it?"

Of course, this is just a pretend story, but it illustrates my point. You see, a little sand can ruin an otherwise perfect cake, just as a few negative comments can ruin an otherwise positive life.

When John and Anne began working on their new relationship they had to change some very powerful negative tapes. Although Anne's mother was a loving, Christian woman, Anne had often heard verbal abuse from her father and of course, John had continued the process of tearing her down. John had to learn to use his words for praise, and Anne had to try and stop listening to the negative tapes that played constantly in her head.

When changing negative tapes it's helpful to understand the ingredients of healthy self-esteem. Dr. Maurice Wagner, a professional Christian counselor and author of

The Sensation of Being Somebody, writes that there are three essential ingredients:

1. A sense of belonging—feeling loved, accepted, cared for, and enjoyed.
2. A sense of self-worth and value—an inner belief that you are of value, that you have something to offer.
3. A sense of being competent—feeling that you can do the task, that you can cope with life.[4]

In other words everyone needs to feel loved, appreciated, and capable. To help achieve this, there are three sentences that need to be said every day to at least one person, preferably to all the people who are close to you—your spouse, children, parents, relatives, and friends. These three crucial sentences are:

- I love you.

- I appreciate you.

- I'm proud of you.

Everyone needs to know that they are loved. By reaching out with words of love, even if the words are not reciprocated, you are making progress in erasing the negative tapes.

At every seminar I give I'm amazed to learn how many women have stopped saying "I love you." It's been years since they've said it or heard it said to them; not because they don't feel it, but because they've gotten out of practice. I know one woman who, at fifty years of age, had never heard a man say that he loved her. I mean *no male,* ever—not her father, brother, grandfather, or her husband. Needless to say, she'd never said it to them either. It was a big risk for her to verbalize her love, but it revolutionized her life. If you've never said it, or have simply gotten out of the habit, it's time to start!

One twelve-year-old girl I know heard me say this and decided to try and tell her father that she loved him. Since she had never said it before, she felt embarrassed and decided that the easiest way to do it was to leave him a note. She put the note on his bed and then went to sleep for the night.

As it happens the girl's mother discovered the note first and thought it was intended for her. She felt the glow of love warm her heart as she read her daughter's childish scrawl. After she finished reading it she put the note on the nightstand.

Later that evening the girl's father came to bed and saw the note on the nightstand. He also assumed it was for him and reading it brought a lump to his throat. The next morning at breakfast, the girl and her parents had a long discussion and they were able to say "I love you" to each other for the first time. It was the beginning of new relationships for all of them.

When Anne first learned about my three-sentence formula, she decided to try it with her children. She got so much positive feedback from them that she began to think about her relationship with her mother. Her mother had always been the one loving person in her life and Anne felt especially close to her, but had never told her so in words.

Anne struggled to muster the courage to speak the words out loud to her mother for the first time. Finally, after a memorable visit in her mother's home (her father was already deceased), she expressed her love, appreciation, and sense of pride to her mother. A short silence ensued as her mother's eyes misted with tears. Finally she said to Anne, "I love you and appreciate you too."

A new and closer relationship began for Anne and her mother, one that she enjoyed until her mother suddenly died about a year later. In hindsight Anne was so thankful that she had voiced her love and appreciation before it was too late.

Doing Positive Things for Yourself

Another important part of renewing your mind is to start doing positive things for yourself. The biggest positive step for Anne was enrolling in college, helping her to rediscover her intelligence and giving her a sense of independence. She also developed many outside interests so that she didn't always dwell on the situation with John.

If you suffer from low self-esteem it may be difficult to do positive things for yourself. When you don't think you're worth it you discount anything that might be good for you. I found that during the period following my divorce, when I felt very unloveable, I had to force myself to get out of the house. If a friend called to ask me to lunch, my first inclination was to refuse. I literally had to make myself accept the invitation. Of course, once I took that positive step, got out of the house, and talked with a friend, I felt much better.

For most women exercise is an extremely beneficial and positive step because exercise produces chemicals in your body that counteract depression. A brisk walk once a day can do a lot for you physically, as well as emotionally. It can definitely help your self-concept. I know of one woman who weathered her own crisis by roller skating! Some days she'd be crying so hard she couldn't stop; literally sobbing just like a small child. But instead of going deeper into despair, she'd put on her roller skates and roll out the driveway onto a nearby jogging trail. Soon she couldn't cry anymore. She'd finish her skating, come back home, and be able to breathe agan. Exercise made all the difference.

If you feel that you're someone else's victim and that person has control over you, exercise is one way to regain some of the control. You may want to start with an attitude that says, "At least no one can stop me from enjoying fresh air and exercising." Yes, it's a small thing, but it's an important positive step.

You should also surround yourself with positive books, magazines, and other reading material. Start by going to your local Christian bookstore and looking for books on self-image and self-esteem. Then, choose the ones that interest you and make time for reading at least a few pages every day. Filling your mind with positive concepts is essential to your continued growth. I would also like to recommend *Virtue* magazine, a Christian publication for women.

Along with this you may wish to see a professional Christian counselor or psychiatrist. Or you may wish to join a Bible study group. Anything that helps you become involved with other people or allows you to express your inner self can be beneficial. I don't think I could have made it through my crisis experience without the wonderful women in my Tuesday night Bible study group. They helped me to realize that I wasn't alone. They offered me help, took me for coffee, and sent weekly notes of love and encouragement. I couldn't feel worthless when I had such terrific women who obviously cared about me.

There are many ways that you can promote your positive growth. One friend of mine found that using correct posture was essential to her healthy self-esteem. Whenever she felt inferior she would make a conscious effort to put her head level, stand as straight as she could, and walk with confidence. She found that when she did this she felt like an entirely different person. When she lifted herself to look more confident, she actually gained confidence. Once while talking with her boss she mentioned that the past year had been really hard for her. Her boss looked surprised and said, "I never would have thought so. You seem to have so much confidence." She couldn't believe it and felt so pleased. Standing tall gave her the extra courage that she needed, even though sometimes she had to consciously remind herself to look up, not down.

Any step you take to raise your self-esteem will be advantageous. Remember that you're a significant person in God's sight. You need to treat yourself accordingly.

Do Something Positive for Others

Not only are you a significant person, but you've got a whole life out there waiting for you, which includes other people. Jesus says in Matthew 22:37–40: "You shall love the LORD your God with all your heart, with all your soul, and with all your mind. This is the first and great commandment. And the second is like it: You shall love your neighbor as yourself. On these two commandments hang all the Law and the Prophets."

In this passage we are commanded to love God and love our neighbor. There are only *two* commandments. We are not *commanded* to love ourselves because that is assumed. We're commanded to love our neighbors.

This is a key point when working on your self-esteem. It's not enough to concentrate on doing only positive things for yourself. You also need to be involved in positive things for others. This doesn't mean being another person's doormat—please notice I said *positive* things, not *anything*.

I love what Dr. D. James Kennedy shared in a sermon on this very subject.

> If loving ourselves becomes the first prerequisite, and developing this image is essential before we can do anything else, we may spend many years doing just that. Suppose after ten years of working on our self-image, we get to the place where we think, "I love myself and I'm really delighted with myself"—and then we die! And God says, "I see that you didn't love your neighbor." We reply, "Well, you see, God, I was intending to do that but I spent

the last ten years working on my self-image. You told me that I can't love my neighbor until I love myself. So I was working on that but you pulled my string too soon!" How do you think that would wash at the Final Judgment?[5]

Do you see the point? We're to love our neighbors, *now.* In working on a healthy self-concept, don't forget that now is the time to work on reconciling any broken or strained relationships, if possible. Now is the time to reach out and help others.

In the past when I was feeling low I forced myself to do something positive for other people. I contacted my church and told them that I was willing to visit church members who were in the hospital. The first Tuesday of every month I called the church and found out the names of the people in the hospital. That week I took a small potted plant and a card to each of them. (I purchased the cards in bulk at the Christian bookstore so it wasn't very expensive.)

I'll have to admit that hospital visitation was a bit frightening at first. After all, I didn't know these people, what would I have to say? Thankfully, all I had to do was ask them about themselves and their families. Before too long we were deep in conversation and I was the one being blessed! At the end of each visit I felt so much better about myself—that's one of the side benefits of sharing yourself with others—and I gained new friends in the process. I learned firsthand that it is not the things we do for ourselves that bring peace and contentment, but the things we do for others. Giving, not getting, brings inner satisfaction and joy.

One woman I know decided to share herself by starting a Bible study for the children in her apartment complex. The children were so excited about this that soon there was a need for *two* Bible study groups, and this woman enlisted the help of her neighbor to lead the second group.

Together they are making an impact in their neighborhood and community.

An elderly woman, who is virtually bedridden because of arthritis in her legs, still has a desire to help others. She also loves animals. Every day she reads the newspaper and concentrates on the "missing pets" section of the classifieds. She then calls all the numbers listed to find out if the people have located their lost animals. If they haven't, she gives them important information that may help locate the animal (such as calling local veterinarians) and gives them the phone numbers of different community groups that keep a list of "found" animals. Her cheerful, encouraging words, along with her valuable knowledge has helped reunite many pet owners with their pets. Even though bedridden, she still makes a difference in people's lives.

Another woman I know, who loves babies but whose children are all grown, has become a foster mother for drug-addicted and abused infants. She is able to give them the love and care they need and also fulfill her own need to be loved, needed, and accepted. It's a wonderful arrangement for all concerned!

Remember, a healthy self-concept allows you to *forget yourself* and concentrate on others. Reaching out to others is God's plan for you and for everyone. Your way of reaching out will be unique because God's plan for you is unlike His plan for anyone else.

Your positive impact will become possible as you develop your self-esteem, the final step toward the goal of a healthy self-concept.

SELF-ESTEEM:
Building
A Positive Self-Concept

*An adequate self-concept
is a precious possession.
It is the premise upon which
a person can devote himself wholeheartedly
to living a useful and productive life.*

—Dr. Maurice E. Wagner[1]

CHAPTER SIX

In 1967, as the director of a modeling agency, I met many girls and women who were competing in various pageants. Through them I learned about the Mrs. Oregon pageant. Since I had always dreamed of being a pageant winner, my interest was piqued. My self-confidence, however, was weak. The old programming from my childhood came back to me and said, "You'll never be able to compete against all the beautiful women in the pageant. You don't stand a chance. Just forget it."

For some reason I just couldn't forget it. By this time I'd learned that the old childhood programming was sometimes wrong. I knew that having a title like Mrs. Oregon would open doors and provide new opportunities for me. Even though I didn't enter the pageant that year, I decided to at least attend and find out more about it. Watching the 1967 pageant, I just couldn't get the idea of competing out of my mind.

During the next year my confidence and self-esteem grew, and in 1968 I decided to enter the pageant. What a surprise and thrill it was when I was named the winner! It seemed that many of my old fantasies were coming true.

Winning the title also helped to open doors that I hadn't even fantasized about. As Mrs. Oregon 1968 I competed in the Mrs. America pageant which was held in Minneapolis.

Back then the pageant was not strictly a beauty pageant like it is today. Instead, it was a well-rounded homemaker competition. Lasting ten days, the fifty contestants competed in such varied events as money management, cooking, shopping, community involvement, and entertaining. I think the pageant winner could more aptly be named "Superwoman." Although I didn't win the Mrs. America title, the pageant experience was one of the highlights of my life.

The title of Mrs. Oregon also launched my speaking career when the local chapter of the Christian Women's Club asked me to speak at their monthly meeting. For the first time I gave my testimony. My knees were shaking and I asked for the biggest lectern available so that I could hide behind it. I also made sure that the microphone was attached to the lectern so that I didn't have to move!

The Lord blessed that first speaking engagement and the leaders of Christian Women's Club asked if they could put my name on a list of available speakers. Before I knew it I was being asked to speak at different Christian Women's Clubs in Oregon, Washington, Idaho, and California. It was the beginning of a speaking career that has continued to this day.

Through this I've learned that although God has given me talent as a speaker and the desire to speak, it is up to me to believe in myself enough to do it. It isn't enough that I have the desire and the talent, I also have to take *action*. If I had decided not to compete in the Mrs. Oregon pageant, I would never have received the title. Without the title, many other events would never have transpired. Although it has been over twenty years since I was Mrs. Oregon, the title is still with me. In fact, just last week I spoke at a Pat Boone/Bethel celebrity benefit in Chattanooga, Tennessee, and one of the reasons why I was asked to speak was because I had competed in the Mrs. America pageant. For some reason, people want to see what a pageant winner looks and sounds like—even (or especially?) over twenty years later!

As Mrs. Oregon 1968, I experienced what it was like to be a "somebody"—at least in other people's eyes. At the Oregon State Fair that year I was asked to award the prizes to the rodeo contestants. This honor included reserved box seat tickets for my family and me. As my daughter, Deanna, then ten years old, sat in those box seats, right next to all the action, she kept looking back behind her at the people sitting way up at the top of the bleacher section where our family had sat last year. Finally, I asked Deanna why she kept looking back at the bleachers. She replied, "I'm just remembering last year when you were a nobody. I'm sure glad you're a somebody now!"

Yes, it felt good to be a *somebody*. But, the truth was, I'd been a *somebody* all along. I just didn't believe in myself enough to realize it. I didn't need the Mrs. Oregon title, the modeling jobs, or the speaking engagements to make me a somebody. God had already proclaimed my worth by sending His son, Jesus, to die for me. Why hadn't I realized it before? How many other women needed to realize the very same truth in their own lives?

As I contemplated those questions I began to feel stifled in my ability to help women by teaching them about self-improvement through secular means. Helping women to feel confident about themselves through modelling skills felt shallow—good, but not good enough. I knew that without understanding the value God placed on a person's life, all the other improvements would only be temporary band-aids for low self-esteem.

With this in mind I resigned as the director of the modeling agency and began researching my own self-improvement course based on Christian principles. In 1969 I started teaching my own course called, "The Image of Loveliness." The first class was held in my living room—a very humble beginning, but one that God blessed. Eventually, as the course became more and more popular, I formed a corporation called Image Improvement, Inc., which trained consultants to teach the Image Improvement courses throughout the U.S. and internationally. Twenty years later I sold my business to Ron and Jane Barnes, of Camp Hill, Pennsylvania, and I have been retained as a consultant. Although I sometimes miss teaching the course, I am now able to devote all my time to my busy speaking career.

Self-esteem: How You Feel about Yourself

If I've learned anything over the years it's that healthy self-esteem must be nurtured. If Satan can rob us of a positive self-esteem, he can rob us of the wonderful plans God has for us. Attacking our self-esteem is often where Satan will concentrate his efforts. We're usually good at knocking ourselves; it's feeling confident and loving ourselves that seem difficult.

When I'm speaking before a group of women I facetiously ask each of them to stand up and shout out their five best qualities. Invariably, the women in the audience start to titter nervously and look for the nearest exit. Before I lose my whole audience I let them off the hook by telling them I was only kidding. I then continue by saying that if we were really forced to stand up and shout out our five best qualities, most of us would attempt to mumble one or two and then have to sit back down. We'd probably feel guilty and quite "unchristian." We've been conditioned not to believe in ourselves to such an extent that we don't even realize all the wonderful qualities that God has given us. Just to mention them is considered boasting.

On the reverse side, however, we'd be very quick about listing our five worst qualities. In fact, most of us would have a hard time stopping at just five. We often dwell on our negative characteristics while our positive characteristics are downplayed.

If you are suffering from low self-esteem, you should know just what it is costing you. Low self-esteem results in many areas of destruction and defeat, among them victimization, destroyed relationships, a loss of hope for the future, and stunted potential.

The Victim Cycle

The first area of defeat and destruction is the victim cycle, often referred to as codependency. There are many excellent books available on this subject, such as *Love Is A Choice*, by the doctors of the well-known Minirth-Meier Clinic.[2] Victimization is one of the most debilitating and destructive results of low self-esteem.

I read in a recent newspaper article that on an average day, thousands of women worldwide are beaten in their homes by their partners. Thousands more are raped, assaulted, and sexually harassed. Hedy Nuriel, first vice-chairman of the National Coalition of Domestic Violence, said, "For many of us, it's safer to be out on the streets than to be in our own homes."[3]

Every weekend when I conduct my seminars, women share things like:

• Pray that I can be an encourager. My husband is an addict. He has been in a rehabilitation center. I am starting to recover from being a codependent person.

• My husband and I are separated. I can no longer facilitate my husband's addictions which include alcohol and gambling. We have three small children.

• My husband is physically abusive. I pray that the Lord will change him so that our family can be reunited.

Women are being victimized in Christian, as well as non-Christian homes. Any relationship where you are verbally, emotionally, or physically abused victimizes you, and low self-esteem keeps you trapped in the victim's cycle.

Many women are caught in such situations because their husbands are addicted to alcohol or drugs, like Anne's husband, John. These women suffer from self-esteem that is so low they become "non-persons." Unless they are able to break the cycle of victimization, the pattern will repeat itself endlessly. This will lead to further lowering of self-esteem and a widespread destruction of personal relationships.

Destroyed Relationships

John and Anne's relationship was clearly destructive for both of them. Deep inside, John knew his drinking, womanizing, and abusiveness were wrong, so his self-esteem continually dropped. The lousier he felt about himself, the more he belittled Anne to try and make himself feel more important. With John demeaning Anne through his words and ruinous behavior, her self-esteem became even lower. Because she had allowed herself to be John's victim, they had a no-win situation.

Before Anne separated from John, their relationship was being destroyed, along with most of their other personal relationships as well. Their three children, who were then teenagers, began to rebel against their authority, and family life became nonexistent. Anne desperately wanted to be able to help her children, but because she couldn't help herself, there was no way she could help them. One of her sons began experimenting with drugs. Another son stole a car and ended up in jail. Her daughter withdrew, gained a lot of weight, and became severely depressed.

Anne's friends were appalled by what was happening in her life. They tried to help her, talk with her, and motivate her to make a change. In Anne's destructive mode she couldn't even hear them. Although she knew in her heart they were right, it made no impact on her behavior. Eventually she alienated many of her friends and increased her sense of isolation and loneliness.

I can identify with Anne in a lot of ways. While I was going through my divorce I found myself in a real dilemma. I was still reading "how to have a perfect marriage" books, and every one helped to lower my estimation of myself. I kept thinking that if I just kept reading, I'd eventually find the answer that would change my situation. Instead, I was confronted with all the ways that I had failed. This would bring on depression, crying jags, and a feeling of hopelessness. I discovered a lot of information that could keep a marriage strong, but all the information only made me feel more inadequate.

One evening while talking with a dear friend of mine, Diane Hopper, I told her about the most recent marriage book I'd read. With tears streaming down my face, I sobbed about the ways that I had failed. Finally, Diane gently said to me, "It's time to put the books away. Close them up. They aren't going to help you at this point. You're torturing yourself over and over again by dwelling on this type of book." At that moment I realized that she was right. I thank God for such a loving and insightful friend. She helped me put a stop to the self-destruction.

Along with my friend's wise counsel, I was also helped by the fact that I had good self-esteem at the onset of my crisis experience. I shudder to think what would have happened to me if my self-esteem had been low in the beginning. More than likely I would have rejected my friend's counsel and alienated her through my destructive behavior. It's so easy to get caught in the downward spiral of self-hate which spreads its poison to all personal relationships.

Low self-esteem also destroys your relationship with God. Although you may know that God loves you and you know that you love Him, if you can't stand yourself, you're belittling His creation. Once you begin to criticize the creation, it is easy to eventually start criticizing the Creator, which leads to a serious breakdown in your walk with the Lord.

When your personal relationships are falling apart, and your relationship with God is imperiled, you've come to the next area of destruction wrought by low self-esteem: loss of hope for the future.

A Future Without Hope

Anne felt totally trapped by her situation. She believed her only escape was death. Every day her situation grew more intolerable. She couldn't imagine going on in the same way for another day, let alone years. Since her self-esteem was basically nil, she didn't know that she actually had options.

That's what happens when low self-esteem takes root. After a while you don't believe you have any choices left. You're trapped as a victim in destructive relationships. Most of the time you tell yourself you deserve your situation; if you were just a better person, good things would come your way.

In Anne's life she was desperate enough to contemplate suicide. Before I met her, at one of the internal peaks of her crisis experience, she seriously considered escaping through death. Two people made a difference in her life. At church that week a friend came up to Anne and said, "I believe in you, Anne. You're going to be okay." Three days later, her work supervisor said to her, "Anne, you are a wonderful person."

As Anne tells it: "I remember thinking, 'You're kidding! I'm a wonderful person?' I thought about it for days. My boss hardly knew me, but I thought, 'If she can believe in me, so can I.' The power of words . . . we don't realize that we might stop someone from committing suicide by just a few words."

Knowing that God's plan was neither suicide nor divorce, but not knowing what God really intended for her life, Anne began to think she would just have to exist in a "walking wounded" state. Her life was out of her control. She wanted to gain control, but she didn't know how to do it.

In Numbers, chapters 13 and 14, the Bible tells the story of the Israelites who have been led out of Egypt by Moses and are just on the verge of entering the promised land. They send spies from each tribe into the land to scope things out. They want to know what's in store for them before they make a move.

When the spies return they bring back the fruit of the land to show the people; the land is truly flowing with milk and honey. It's an ideal place except for one thing: the people already living there are strong and have fortified cities. Nevertheless, two of the spies, Caleb and Joshua, recommend immediately seizing the land. They believe that the Israelites are well able to overcome any obstacles.

The other spies, however, said, "We are not able to go up against the people, for they are stronger than we. . . . There we saw the giants . . . and we were like grasshoppers in our own sight, and so we were in their sight."[4]

In Numbers 14:1–2 the Bible goes on to say, "Then all the congregation lifted up their voices and cried, and the people wept that night. And all the children of Israel murmured against Moses and Aaron, and the whole congregation said to them, 'If only we had died in the land of Egypt! Or if only we had died in this wilderness.'"

The Israelites, feeling like grasshoppers—not believing in themselves or God's plan for their future—wished they were dead. Because of their self-esteem and their complaining against God, they spent forty years wandering around in the wilderness before their children actually received all God had planned.

The Israelites, through their lack of belief in God and themselves, had a future without hope. Their low self-esteem deprived them of the one thing in life they really wanted. None of those who complained ever entered the promised land, only Caleb, Joshua, and the next generation of Israelites.

Things haven't changed much today. Your self-esteem can keep you locked in a future without hope. When I was a cannery worker, even though it was a high-paying job, I felt trapped and without a future. The endless assembly line of cans, the machinery droning, the exhaustion of the night shift, all contributed to my sense of being trapped. Often, just like Anne or the Israelites, I longed for a new life, but I just didn't know how to achieve it. Not believing in myself or my abilities, I was in a pit created by my low self-esteem. My potential was being stunted.

Stunted Potential

As a high school and college student my favorite subject was speech. I loved getting up in front of an audience and sharing information with them. It felt right, and after all, I *had* to do it—it was a class assignment! When I got older I just couldn't translate that classroom experience into real life. My low self-esteem caused me to doubt my abilities. If someone asked me to speak to a group of women at church, I felt totally inadequate and declined the request.

In hindsight I can see that I wasted so many years, but I had to first realize my God-given potential. It didn't matter that I had the talent to be a speaker all along. It didn't matter that I even had the interest and enthusiasm. It didn't matter because I didn't believe in myself enough to actually do it. I always figured somebody else could do it better.

As a young girl I also had artistic talent. I even won a

few blue ribbons for drawing contests in junior high and high school. After high school, however, I didn't pick up a paintbrush or sketch pad for twenty-five years. Not until my crisis experience did I finally take my first oil painting class. Rediscovering my talent was great therapy but it's so sad that I wasted all the years in-between.

After a long time I realized that my low self-esteem was stunting my God-given potential. I thought that to use my talents I had to be the best speaker or artist in the world. I had to learn that God didn't require me to be the *best* in the world; only that I develop my skills and be *the best that I could be* with the talents He had given me. He just wanted me to fulfill my potential.

Before Anne married John, she had been a gifted scholar. Her I.Q. score was in the genius level. She attended two years of college on a scholarship, but dropped out to marry John. As John began to verbally abuse her, she started to doubt her intelligence and abilities. Being told on a daily basis that she was worthless and dumb obviously had a very debilitating effect on her self-esteem. Consequently, Anne withdrew from life in many ways, including pursuing her education and using her great intelligence. She even began to consider herself quite stupid. She figured it was just a fluke that she'd done so well on the I.Q. test and even gotten into college at all. She lost sight of the wonderful potential within her. Once she stopped the flow of her God-given talents and potential, she felt even more worthless, which added impetus to the already swirling whirlpool that was drowning her self-esteem.

By stunting her potential she let Satan win the battle, just as we all do when we waste the talents God has given us. By not using God's gifts to us, we not only hurt ourselves, but grieve God. God loves you, created you, and has great plans for your life. Unfortunately, you may miss out on these plans because of low self-esteem.

The Plague of Comparison

One of the ways we feed our low self-esteem and stunt our potential is to compare ourselves with others. Comparison is like the plague—it infects our self-esteem and destroys everything in its path.

Have you compared yourself lately? Maybe you've said: "Oh, she's so much thinner than I am." Or "Boy, I wish I could do that." These comparisons can destroy your self-esteem.

When I competed in the Mrs. America pageant in 1968, there was a judged event called "child communication" that involved getting on a stage and communicating for five minutes with a child under the age of five whom you had never met before. The rules allowed you to use a prop, but it couldn't cost more than one dollar. I racked my brain for an appropriate prop and came up with the bright idea of using an animal. The day before the judging I scoured Minneapolis for a kitten. Eventually I found one in a local pet store and after explaining the situation, the owner agreed that I could bring the kitten back the following day after the event.

Since it was summertime in Minneapolis and very warm, they held the child communication event at an outdoor amphitheater. When I arrived I realized I couldn't put the kitten down because it might run away and I'd never see it again. Of course, everything was delayed, and by the time I actually got on the stage the kitten was very fidgety and nervous. I tried my best to hold onto it while the little girl came and sat by me in the middle of the stage.

By this time the kitten was obviously distressed, so I asked the little girl what she would do if this were her little kitty. Without hesitation she said, "Well, I'd give it back!" So much for my bright idea!

Desperate to try and make contact with this little girl, I

said, "Well, wouldn't you treat this kitty like your mother would treat you if you were having a bad day? Wouldn't you maybe sing to it?" She thought about it for a moment and started to feel sorry for the kitten. In that moment she forgot all about the huge audience and had eyes only for the kitten. All of a sudden she started to sing to it. She sang on and on and on. Pretty soon the bell rang and my five minutes were up! I placed fourth in that competition because of her!

The next contestant to compete was "Mrs. Washington." She came on stage and sat down with a little boy. He would not even acknowledge that she existed. She tried many different things but nothing worked. In fact, toward the end of the five minutes he got up from the chair and started to go down the stairs to find his mother.

Just before he reached the stairs, Mrs. Washington caught him. She tapped him on the shoulder and said, "Hey, what's the matter? Have I done something wrong?" He whirled around, looked her right in the eye, and loudly answered, "Yes! How come I didn't get a kitty like Cynthia got?"

That about broke up the audience. It was one of the funniest things that happened during the pageant. Every time I think about it, I have to chuckle, but I've also learned a lesson—that little boy was extremely unhappy because he compared himself with Cynthia. He missed out on all the fun things Mrs. Washington had planned because he kept thinking about what Cynthia got. How often do we do the same thing? How often do we miss out on God's plans for our lives because we're too busy concentrating on what He gave to someone else?

Being raised in a conservative Christian home, I was never allowed to go to movies until Billy Graham started making them! I'll never forget the first Billy Graham movie I saw because Colleen Townsend was in it. My dreams of Elizabeth Taylor were replaced by a much-improved role model! Colleen was so beautiful, and I used to wish that someday I could meet her.

My teenage wish came true when I was asked to speak at a women's conference being held at Grace Community Church in Phoenix, Arizona. I would be sharing the platform with two other speakers. One of them was Colleen Townsend, now Colleen Townsend Evans. Of course I said yes. I was so excited! I could hardly believe it, until I started to really think about it. *Oh, no,* I thought, *Everyone knows Colleen Townsend Evans. Who's Joanne Wallace? I can't speak at the same conference with her!*

I began to worry and fret to such an extent that I almost called and canceled the day before the conference. Comparing myself with Colleen was literally making me ill. I had to pull myself together. I knew that my talk was prepared and that God had a plan for me. I also knew that if I didn't go, my personal self-esteem would go down the tubes.

I wish now that I hadn't spent so much time worrying. Attending and speaking at that conference was wonderful. Everything went so well and meeting Colleen Townsend Evans was a thrill. We had a chance to get to know each other and even went shopping at a thrift store together! I discovered that she is a real, caring person—even better than the movies! I'm so glad I didn't let comparison stop me from experiencing one of the greatest blessings I've ever received.

My friend, Anne, was also infected by the plague of comparison. As she looked around at the women in her church, they seemed to have it all together. She saw them laughing and socializing, and felt jealous. In her mind she couldn't join them because she feared they'd discover that she was a failure. They might find out that she didn't have a perfect marriage and a wonderful husband. They might find out she was stupid. She couldn't risk their rejection, so she silently watched them and compared herself endlessly.

Of course, this only deepened her sense of failure and further lowered her self-esteem.

Another devious way that comparison spreads its poison is in causing you to compare yourself with someone else and feel *superior*. Healthy self-esteem neither underestimates nor overestimates personal worth. As Paul warns in Romans 12:3: "For I say, through the grace given to me, to everyone who is among you, not to think of himself more highly than he ought to think, but to think soberly, as God has dealt to each one a measure of faith."

Remember, healthy self-esteem makes you feel equal to everyone else. It frees you from feeling superior or inferior. It's like the sign that a group of young boys hung on their clubhouse which read:

> Nobody act too big.
> Nobody act too small.
> Everybody act *medium*.

We need to get rid of comparison in our lives so that we can all act *medium*.

One very appropriate Scripture verse that deals with comparison is Galatians 6:4. It's a good one to memorize as an antidote when you find yourself being infected by the plague of comparison. "Let everyone be sure that he is doing his very best, for then he will have the personal satisfaction of work well done, and won't need to compare himself with someone else" (Living Bible).

In order to feel good about ourselves, we've got to put forth our best effort. This truth can be applied in very small but practical ways. Have you ever gone to the grocery store looking just awful? You probably figured you'd just run in to get a loaf of bread and no one would see you. However, if you're like me, that's exactly the time you run into someone for whom you'd really like to look good! I'm not suggesting that you have to wear a dress and high heels to the grocery store, but it's important to feel good about yourself so that you can relax and talk to people, and not do a disappearing act under the grocery cart!

When we've done our best we're then able to concentrate on others—the ultimate goal. Low self-esteem is such a deadly weapon used by Satan because it keeps us from reaching out to others and being fully used by God.

What happened when Anne found new self-worth by understanding God's love for her, seeing herself as God did, and then translating that image into her feelings? All of these positive changes in Anne's life had a powerful influence on John. While separated from him, she continued to assure him that she loved him and ultimately wanted their marriage to be reconciled, but only when and if he sought help. For a while, John just bided his time and waited for her to come back. When she didn't, he began to take a long, hard look at his own life. God began dealing with him, and although he was resistant at first, John finally decided to seek professional help through Alcoholics Anonymous and a Christian counselor. Through almost two years of hard work, time spent in prayer, and the help of professional counselors, John and Anne are now back together, working on a strong and equal relationship.

A reconciliation may not be possible in your situation, but you can always start over again, as I did. Once you're on the road to a healthy self-concept, you'll find yourself ready to tackle the next hurdle to starting over: learning to trust again.

TRUST:
Taking the Risk Again

*If you approach each new person you meet
in a spirit of adventure,
you will find yourself endlessly fascinated
by the new channels of thought and experience
and personality that you encounter.*

—Eleanor Roosevelt[1]

CHAPTER SEVEN

Whenever I've been hurt deeply, I experience the overwhelming desire to hide myself away in some remote cabin. I long to lead a hermit's life. I envision living in a cabin located next to a serene lake, complete with a lush garden full of fresh green vegetables, red radishes, and tomatoes. And no other person lives near me. It sounds like paradise—peace, beauty, and best of all—no one to hurt me again. Possibly you've felt like this as well. I think it's a common feeling when you've suffered deep emotional pain. You'll see the same pattern in nature when hurt animals instinctively hole up in a quiet, peaceful place in order to nurse their wounds. This is often the best way to promote the healing process.

A period of time spent nursing your wounds may be necessary for your healing process, but a total withdrawal from life is not the answer. No matter how hurt, rejected, or worthless you may feel, closing yourself off to future relationships won't help. As a human being you were created by God with the desire to love and be loved. Shutting yourself off from other people is slow suicide. As C. S. Lewis said:

> To love at all is to be vulnerable. Love anything, and
> your heart will certainly be wrung and possibly broken. If

you want to make sure of keeping it intact, you must give it to no one, not even an animal. Wrap it carefully round with hobbies and little luxuries; avoid all entanglements; lock it up safe in the casket or coffin of your selfishness. But in that casket—safe, dark, motionless, airless—it will change. It will not be broken; it will become unbreakable, impenetrable, irredeemable. The only place outside Heaven where you can be perfectly safe from all the dangers of love is hell.[2]

Love is never completely safe. When you love you take risks; but the alternative—a life without love—is so much worse.

If you're starting over, I assume that you've lost an important relationship in your life. Your loss may have come through death, divorce, moving to a new city, employment change, children grown and leaving home, or even children who are "gone" through substance abuse or running away from home. No matter what caused the loss, chances are you've lost at least one important relationship. This loss brings with it extreme pain and the reluctance to risk loving or trusting again, and may also bring a sense of rejection.

After my divorce I thought I was rejected for a lifetime and no one could ever love me again. My sense of hurt went so deep that I had difficulty performing simple tasks like putting on my makeup or getting dressed in the morning. What was the point? In my mind, no one cared about me, not even me. Some days I literally didn't do *anything*. The hurt caused me to withdraw from life in many ways. I know now that this is not an uncommon reaction. My friend, Sandra, also experienced this withdrawal, although for a different reason.

Sandra and her husband raised four children. Motherhood represented over thirty years of Sandra's life, so my friend experienced a crisis when her youngest daughter left home to live on her own at age twenty. Sandra, at age fifty-one, experienced the "empty nest" syndrome with intensity. Although she supported her children's independence, the realization that they were all grown and living on their own brought a deep sense of pain and rejection. Although her children did not, in fact, reject her, she still felt useless, unwanted, and unneeded.

During this time Sandra questioned her own purpose in life. Like many women before her, she had difficulty adjusting to the fact that motherhood was no longer her primary role. Even though her husband tried to help her, he couldn't seem to understand the depth of her sense of loss. To him, having the children gone was a bonus as well as a loss. Now he and Sandra would have the freedom to travel and do things together as never before.

For Sandra, her husband's seeming insensitivity created a lack of trust in her relationship with him. She wanted him to be sympathetic and supportive. Instead, he tried to cajole her into a better frame of mind and became angry when she didn't respond. Sandra's reaction was to have her own private pity party. Distrusting her husband's concern for her, she nursed her wounds to such an extent that she was absorbed in feeling sorry for herself. This only led to depression, which aggravated the already adversely affected relationship she had with her husband. Instead of wanting to go out and do things with him, she found excuses for staying home, sometimes never changing out of her bathrobe all day long.

This went on for a couple of months, until Sandra heard her pastor preach an excellent sermon on trust. Through this message she realized that she had been avoiding her husband because she wanted to escape being hurt further. Feeling rejected and sorry for herself, she chose withdrawal from life as the solution. She mistakenly believed that distancing herself from all her personal relationships would alleviate her sense of rejection. Unfortunately, it only made matters worse.

Sandra had to come to terms with her new role in life: a mother with grown, independent children. She now had to focus her energies elsewhere. This renewed energy was launched when she realized two important aspects of rejection.

1. Rejection (or failure) is not a disgrace but just another aspect of life.
2. Rejection (or failure) is an opportunity to learn and can be the seed for new growth.

Part of Sandra's new growth came when she committed herself to spending more time with her husband, building their relationship together. Immediately, this helped to alleviate the loneliness she had faced since her youngest daughter left home.

Lack of Trust Breeds Loneliness

If you've chosen to withdraw from life, hoping that you'll save yourself further pain, you're probably well acquainted with your new source of pain—loneliness. The sharp, aching sensation that often accompanies loneliness is one of the saddest feelings in the world. The more intimate the relationship that was lost or broken, the more intense the loneliness that accompanies it.

Loneliness doesn't necessarily mean you're alone. Possibly you feel lonely in a crowd of people. Or maybe you're lonely even when you're with a group of friends. You may even feel lonely in your closest personal relationships. To understand this, let's look at the most common sources of loneliness.

Loneliness comes:

- when you're separated from cherished friends or relatives.

- through nostalgic memories of the past that will never occur again.

- at particular times of the year.

- when you feel forgotten or rejected.

My friend, Lily, was sixty-two years old when Richard, her husband of forty years, was killed in an automobile accident. For many months after his death Lily didn't know what to do with herself. Understandably, she was overwhelmed with loneliness. In fact, all four of the causes of loneliness listed above collided in her life. She was separated from Richard by death, she spent much of her time dwelling on her past memories of him, special holiday times made the loneliness worse, and as time went by, she felt forgotten by her friends. Where once she and Richard had socialized with other couples on a regular basis, these couples no longer invited just her. She was a single in a social set of doubles. Losing Richard changed almost everything in her life, and the feeling of loneliness was unbearable.

I can identify with Lily's loneliness. After my divorce the sense of loneliness was oppressive. Not only was I lonely, but also alone in a great big house. I didn't trust very many things at that point. I was very vulnerable and easily frightened. At night I jumped at every creak or strange noise I heard. It was definitely not a time of joyous, victorious Christian living. I was being drained of all my energy by loneliness, lack of trust, and fear. I had to learn to combat my loneliness by renewing my energy and purpose in life; *I had to make a conscious decision.*

Through prayer I committed myself to continuing my speaking ministry. I knew that Satan wanted to defeat me by making sure that I never shared God's message with another group of women. I also knew that God had called me to minister to these women. Through Him, I had to overcome my debilitating sense of rejection and loneliness.

Some people try to escape loneliness through tranquilizers, alcohol, or other drugs. Others find more constructive help by going for walks, visiting a friend, listening to music, or reading a good book. As obvious as it sounds, eating right and being physically active can help relieve loneliness. Getting out of the house is vital. Being physically active doesn't necessarily mean exercise. It may mean just getting out and doing *something*.

My widowed friend, Lily, was a former high school teacher. To combat her loneliness after her husband's death, she took a few courses at a local college, which allowed her to start teaching again. About two years after Richard's death she was once again teaching at a Christian high school. Surrounded by young people, with a purpose for her days, she found renewed energy.

Around this time her loneliness was eased considerably by Eric, a wonderful seventy-year-old man whom she met at church. Eric's first wife had died a few years earlier and like Lily, he chose not to withdraw from life, but to embrace it. An active, athletic man, Eric still did over 100 push-ups every day! Lily found him very attractive, and another year later they were married. As Lily put it: "We're not getting married out of loneliness or just for companionship. We're in love!"

I have every reason to believe that Lily is telling the truth. One day, about two years after their marriage, I was in my car waiting for the stoplight to change when I noticed Eric and Lily's car also waiting on the other side of the intersection. I was delighted to see that although the car had bucket seats, Lily was sitting on the hump in the middle, nuzzled as close to Eric as she could get! Take away the gray hair and they looked just like a pair of teenage lovers!

I'm so glad that Lily took the risk and developed a close

relationship with Eric after she lost her first husband. She learned that to beat loneliness you've got to invest time in making new relationships.

In Lily's case it happened that her new relationship also brought a new husband, but this is not always the goal! Building new and trusting relationships does not necessarily mean a relationship with the opposite sex. In fact, if you're married and your husband is not available as a close friend, I believe your friendships should be based with other women. Sharing yourself with someone of the opposite sex, unless that person is your mate, opens up the possibility of an affair, which, of course, should be avoided.

I was able to establish new, close relationships through the women's Bible study group that my church was just beginning to form. Since I was feeling reluctant about reaching out to other people, and the group needed a place to meet, I decided to have the meetings in my home. Otherwise, with my busy schedule I knew I'd have the best intentions to attend but that something could distract me. Hosting the Bible study group in my home guaranteed that I'd have to attend each week! I've never regretted this decision.

We all need and want at least one intimate friendship. If you've built barriers to intimacy in your own life, this chapter and the next one will show you ways to break down those barriers. You don't have to stay in lonely isolation.

To begin with, how is your relationship with God? Are you getting to know Him better? With Christ you can have an intimate, unfailing relationship. You may feel lonely, but with Christ you are never alone. During my crisis experience, the time I spent reading God's Word in daily devotions was my main source of strength as I dealt with loneliness. I also attended the Wednesday night prayer meeting at my church. Although sometimes I didn't *feel* like praying, I did it anyway. Time spent communing with God helped heal the sense of isolation. Through this I've learned that deep loneliness can only be filled by God Himself. A close relationship with Him can meet your needs and ease your loneliness, but as in any close relationship, this requires trust.

Learning to Trust God

When we are in the midst of a crisis situation we may feel disconnected from God, betrayed by Him, and refuse to trust Him. We turn our lives into fortresses because we don't want anyone, including God, getting near us. We build walls and we build them high.

Often we throw prayers over our high walls, asking God to help us, but we don't invite God or anyone else into our fortress. Why? Because we're too afraid. We resist the intimacy we need because we desperately fear being hurt again. In our lonely fortresses we know that God loves us, but instead of trusting Him, we say, "Prove it."

We need to realize that God has proven it. When He sent His Son, Jesus, to die on the cross for us, He proved His love once and for all. Now He says, "Trust Me."

In order to trust God you've got to stop measuring God's trustworthiness by the evidence you can *see*. You cannot measure God's trustworthiness on the basis of past or present hurts. You may never know the exact reasons why God allowed something to happen. You may not always have the answers. But this does not mean that God has failed you. If I'm sure of one thing, it's this: God does not know *how* to fail you.

Sometimes God doesn't let you understand something because it is too heavy for you to bear. Later, when and if the time is right and you can bear it, He'll let you understand. Until then, He wants you to leave it with Him and let Him take care of it. To help me remember this truth, I use the phrase, "put it high on the shelf for now."

I have some friends whose thirteen-year-old daughter

was killed in a freak sledding accident. Devastated by the loss of their only daughter, they experienced overwhelming grief. The burden of just getting through each day was enough to bear. Trying to understand God's overall purpose and plan in their daughter's death was beyond their ability at the time. They had to trust God without knowing all the answers.

There are times in our lives when we have to trust God without knowing all the answers. Our human tendency is to blame Him for the tragedies we experience. Although it is easy to blame God for the result of man's sin, we must remember that God is not the originator of sin, He is not the One who has failed. In fact, our relationship with God is the only unfailing relationship we can have on this earth.

The Scriptures tell us over and over again to trust in God. Psalm 62:8 says, "Trust in Him at all times, you people; pour out your heart before Him; God is a refuge for us." I love this verse because it tells me that not only should I trust God, but *He* is my refuge—I don't need my self-made fortress!

If you're having difficulty trusting God, I want to encourage you to spend time with Him, even if you don't feel like it. Trust, like forgiveness, is a conscious choice. You have the power to decide which way your life will go. Are you going to keep building your walls or allow God to be your fortress?

During my lifetime I've had periods when I've felt distant from God. At those times I've found help in my own prayer journal. When I've doubted God's plan I've been able to reread pages in my journal that document God's great faithfulness. My memory is sometimes short and fallible, but what I've written in my prayer journal is my personal history book that sets the facts straight and provides a great refresher course.

If you don't already have a prayer journal, I would encourage you to start one. Use it to jot down your thoughts, prayer requests, answers to prayer, and also what God says to you during your time spent with Him. Seeing God's faithfulness written in your own words can be so beneficial as you learn to trust Him.

I've also found that when my trust is weak, I must seek help from someone whose faith in God is strong. My former pastor, Tom Wilson, was just such a person. He helped me to remain strong in my trust and love for the Lord, even when my life was in ruins. Despite my natural instinct to build a high fortress, I've found that the best way to overcome loneliness and a lack of trust is to reach out to God and to other people as well.

For some people, learning to trust God is easier than reaching out and trusting another human being. As one woman said, "It's easy to trust Someone who is perfect—it's all those imperfect people I can do without!" The only problem with her statement is that she really *can't* do without other people, as imperfect as they may be. We need each other. Most of us are longing for a close, intimate, loving relationship with at least one person. I'm not talking about a sexual relationship. The best definition I've heard of a truly intimate relationship goes like this:

> An intimate relationship is one in which I feel safe revealing hopes, dreams, fears and the past—including sins and mistakes. In an intimate relationship I can share these things without the fear of being judged, condemned or straightened out.[3]

If we all want this kind of intimate relationship, why don't we all have it? Often it's because we're afraid to risk trusting someone else. Instead, we erect barriers.

Barriers to Trust

One of the basic barriers to developing trust is the fear of appearing foolish. We are often afraid that if we share ourselves with others, they'll laugh. We feel ashamed of being who we are, of being human. Instead, we wear masks to disguise what we really feel.

We need to realize that while our life experiences may be different, we all share the same emotions, fears, and dreams. The fear of appearing foolish is unfounded since everybody is surprisingly alike when the masks are off. As Pablo Casals once said, "The main thing in life is not to be afraid to be human."

Most of us want to wear our "best face" mask at all times. Therefore, we don't allow others to know we are hurting or need help. We just don't trust that they'll understand our pain.

I grew up in an era when you were taught not to share your feelings. I could never admit, for example, that I was depressed, angry, or feeling inferior. I was taught to always bring my "best face" to a situation. If I ever felt angry or sad, I believed it wasn't "Christian." By the time I was a teenager I had learned to mask many common emotions. I was afraid that if someone knew how I really felt inside, I'd be branded as spiritually unfit. I've since learned that putting on a "best face" is often a result of wrong programming and all too often leads to a life filled with secrecy and deception. You *cannot* have an open, intimate relationship if you wear only your best face before others.

Looking back on my own wrong programming, I now understand that God created us with the whole gamut of emotions and there are no feelings which in themselves are spiritually wrong. In fact, God Himself experiences sadness, anger, jealousy—the same emotions we do. Isaiah 53:3 calls Jesus, "A man of sorrows and acquainted with grief." Judges 10:7 speaks of God's anger against Israel, and Exodus 20:5 says, "For I, the LORD your God, am a jealous God." God understands our emotions because we were created in His image.

Of course, we don't always deal with our emotions in

the perfect way that God does; nevertheless, it's heart-breaking when children are taught to hide their natural human emotions. In our society, for example, boys are taught not to cry or share tender emotions. What a pitiful way to stunt human development and create more barriers to trust.

Often, people are taught to be strong and silent, never letting others know that they're fallible. These strong, silent types often end up being involved in secretive sin. Take, for example, various well-known Christian personalities. When the lid is taken off the garbage can of their secret life and the sin is finally exposed, a whole community is in a state of shock. It's time we realized that being the strong, silent type is no longer a compliment.

At my seminars many women have shared their childhood experiences with me—women who, like me, learned to suppress feelings of anger, unhappiness, or inadequacy. They were told, "You shouldn't feel that way."

Through this wrong programming these women grew up with all kinds of negative feelings stuffed down deep inside. As adults we're now handicapped in our ability to have a trusting relationship because we're afraid to share our negative feelings. We need to realize a very simple, but profound, truth: Feelings are *always* all right.

Until you realize this and get in touch with your true feelings, you'll always have trouble trusting. Why? Because building any kind of relationship is difficult when you're wearing a mask. Inevitably, one day the mask will slip, and you'll be left in a relationship built on deception.

When I was growing up I didn't feel close to my only brother, Keith, who is five years my senior. Part of this distance was due to the age difference, but part of it was due to the fact that we were never taught to share openly and honestly with each other. Keith and his wife, Marilyn, are now mental health therapists and, since my divorce, Keith has been encouraging me to open up and share my feelings, even unpleasant ones, with him. He has often told me that the only way we can become close is by sharing our true selves, warts and all. In order to do this, I have to take my mask off.

As the months and years have gone by I've gotten closer and closer to Keith. A turning point in our relationship occurred when Keith did something that really hurt my feelings. Although Keith didn't know I was upset, and I tried to suppress it, I just couldn't get over it. Finally, I decided to take Keith's advice. If he wanted me to share myself, openly and honestly, I would.

That day I wrote Keith a letter and told him that I was feeling upset with him. Writing that letter represented a very big risk for me, and I was afraid of what his response would be. What if he slammed the door on further communication with me? What if he only wanted me to share negative feelings as long as they didn't have to do with him personally? I hoped and prayed that Keith would still be willing to talk with me.

Keith came through for me with flying colors. After receiving my letter he wrote a wonderful letter in reply. He let me know that he was very happy that I had shared what I was feeling with him. He confirmed that being open and honest was the best way to resolve a problem. I'm so thankful that we are now working together to have the close relationship we once missed. Through this I've learned that a relationship built on honesty is worth the risks involved.

In order to build an honest, trusting relationship, you've got to know how you're really feeling. This may require that you take a good look inside yourself. Take the time to stop and quietly meditate on what you are feeling most strongly. Is it anger? Sadness? Longing? Elation? Whatever it is, identifying it by name will help you know how to deal with it. Often we react on the basis of our feelings without taking the time to identify them.

After you identify your feelings you'll be able to share them with someone else in a way that is beneficial. By identifying your emotion, you're using rational thought, which helps you to be in control of your emotions rather than your emotions controlling you. Remember, it doesn't matter if your feelings are positive or negative—they're always all right. It's only the way that you *express* a particular feeling that may be wrong.

If, for example, you've had a very busy day and you're feeling stressed and upset when you come home from work, the feelings of stress and distress in themselves are not wrong but what you *do* with the feelings determines any right or wrong action.

In this example I can see three distinct choices. You can either stuff your feelings and pretend that nothing is wrong (all the while pushing the turmoil deeper inside you); you can vent your distress on whoever is home by yelling, nagging, or otherwise ruining their day too; or you can express your feelings by saying, "I've had a very stressful day. It's not your fault, but I feel very upset right now."

Pretend That Nothing Is Wrong

Suppressing your feelings and pretending that nothing is wrong is usually chosen in a futile effort to make the feelings go away. Unfortunately, suppressing your feelings won't make them go away. Somehow, someway, feelings are always expressed.

Research reveals that suppressing feelings only makes your body's reaction to those feelings more pronounced[4] and can even cause physical illness. I've had several people relate their link between suppressed inner turmoil and developing ulcers of the stomach. Researchers are beginning to suggest that cancer is sometimes associated with bitterness or stress. Your feelings are very powerful and will express themselves even at your body's expense.

Feelings will always come out—either by talking about

them or through actions, in conscious or subconscious ways. Have you ever been so happy you just couldn't hide a big, wide, ridiculous-looking grin? Or so sad you couldn't stop yourself from crying no matter how hard you bit your lip or tried to swallow the lump in your throat? If so, you know how powerful your emotions can be.

Act Out Your Feelings

Whether or not you should choose the second option depends on whether your feelings are positive or negative. Acting on positive feelings such as love or gratitude will most likely produce positive results. Acting on negative feelings, however, will usually produce negative results. Slamming your fist through a window to act out your anger is not very constructive for you or the window!

I know a young college girl who became so upset about her relationship with a boyfriend and some of the girls in her dorm that she actually put her fist through her dorm room window. The girl almost bled to death because she severed the primary artery in her arm as she pulled her arm back through the jagged glass. This sophomore temporarily lost all use of her hand and a full semester of college because of her action. She'd have been wiser to express her anger verbally to a school counselor, friend, or parent.

Express Your Feelings Verbally

Instead of suppressing or acting out your feelings, the most appropriate way is to talk about them. Verbalizing allows your feelings to come out in the open where you can deal with them. While suppressing or acting out your feelings may cause more problems, expressing them verbally releases them.

While working on this book, my daughter, Deanna, had a chance to put into practice this very point when my nine-year-old grandson, Aron, came home from school. Obviously something was wrong; the moment he walked in he slammed the front door behind him. Throwing his backpack full of books on the floor, he began to angrily march upstairs. Deanna, taking Aron's not so subtle hints, said, "Aron, what's wrong?"

"Nothing," said Aron as he stomped up a few more stairs.

"Did something happen at school?"

"I don't know."

"Well, why don't you come down into my bedroom where we can talk about it privately?"

Reluctantly, Aron slowly came down the stairs and followed Deanna into her room to sit on the bed next to her. Having just seen a display of his anger, she said to him, "I guess you must feel angry. I know what that's like. It really makes you want to kick something. But, it is very important that you talk about your anger so that it doesn't come out in destructive ways. Do you think you can tell me how you feel?"

Hearing this, Aron's defensive anger began to melt. Since Deanna had validated his feelings without making him feel foolish, he was then able to get to the heart of his frustration by saying, "I don't like myself. I feel that everyone else is better than me today."

With this very vulnerable statement the door was open for Deanna to have an intimate talk with Aron. Apparently, the other kids in Aron's class were teasing him about wearing glasses and being the class "brain." One of the girls tried to help by saying that Aron "would be cute without his glasses," but since he wore glasses all the time, this cuteness was unattainable! Feeling unattractive and rejected, Aron was ready to hear Deanna tell him just how special he was in so many ways, even though sometimes, like everyone else, he might feel inferior. Deanna even listed some of the important men who wear glasses, including John Denver, Steven Spielberg, and Aron's dad!

Following their heart-to-heart talk, Aron began feeling

very bubbly and happy because he'd been able to release his feelings of inferiority and anger in an appropriate way. The next morning when he came down to breakfast, the first thing he said was: "Mom, wasn't our talk good? It's just so good to talk about our feelings!"

Aron and Deanna are learning an important lesson in trust and intimacy, one that I hope they'll never forget. They're learning to share their feelings honestly and openly with each other. Yes, it involves a risk, but the reward of an intimate relationship far outweighs the risk of getting hurt.

Feelings should always be validated. Many people would not need to be in therapy if others validated their feelings. Whether you agree or disagree with the person's feelings isn't the issue. Just hearing "I can understand your feelings," or "It's all right to feel that way" is the important message.

Learning to share your feelings openly and honestly is such a significant part of building a trusting relationship. But this may be difficult to do if you feel that the circumstances in your life have left you without any options.

You Always Have Choices

If you've been confronted with a major life crisis, you may believe that your whole life is beyond your control. Yet even in the most desperate situations, you still have choices. I can illustrate this point through a minor incident that happened to me several years ago.

Since I travel almost every weekend for various speaking engagements, I am well acquainted with commercial airlines. Although most of my trips go smoothly, I've also had a few problems. One time I went to the ticket counter, ticket in hand, to receive my seat assignment, only to be told that the flight had been overbooked and there would not be room for me.

When this happened I felt very upset and angry. I had to

make the flight so that I could get home to my family, yet it seemed I had no choice in the matter. I blamed the airlines for taking my choice away and went to wait for another flight in the waiting area. Feeling powerless, I berated the airlines for conspiring against me. It took several minutes before I began to see that I still had some control over the situation.

First, I could stay in the waiting room fuming at the unfairness of it all. Or, I could regain some control by finding out as much as I could about the practice of overbooking flights.

With new determination I went to seek out an airline official. When I was introduced to him I didn't vent my frustration in a tirade against the airlines. Instead, very calmly, I asked him what he could tell me about the policy of overbooking flights, and more importantly, was it legal to do so? After much hemming and hawing on his part I found out some very enlightening information. Although strictly speaking the overbooking policy was legal, there were also guidelines that stated airlines had to get me on another flight within a short period of time or I was entitled to a free flight with reimbursement for my ticket.

Three hours later I was on another flight with the money for my ticket in my wallet. There was at least some compensation for an unpleasant situation because I decided to make a positive choice in my predicament.

This same attitude came to my aid during my crisis experience. Although I couldn't erase the fact that my marriage was devastated or that my company owed back taxes and was being sued or that I was hobbling around on crutches with torn ligaments in my ankle, I could still have some measure of control over my situation by using my crisis as a learning experience. I couldn't make the problems disappear, but I could grow by getting in touch with my feelings and talking about them. Ultimately, I could also choose to risk sharing them with someone else in a new relationship.

This book is part of that risk. Before I could allow my experience to be shared on these pages, I had to start slowly, building a new foundation for trust and honesty in my life. If I'd stayed behind the barriers and walls I'd built, this book would never have become a reality. The walls didn't come down overnight. They started to crumble little by little as I took small risks.

Begin with Small Risks

Unlike many feelings, trust doesn't come instantly. In large measure trust is a culmination of time and history between two people. You begin to trust when someone has proven worthy of trust.

At first I would recommend taking small risks as you try to rebuild trust. Choose your confidant very carefully. There are limits to what you should risk sharing until you're sure the other person can keep a confidence. Start by revealing things you don't mind if someone else knows. The old saying, "Once burned, twice careful," has some merit here.

You should also keep in mind that sharing yourself is more than venturing an opinion. You don't really share yourself until you share your feelings. Stating an opinion such as, "I'm against abortion," is nothing unique. It's when you're able to tell how you *feel* about abortion and the events in your life that led you to your opinion that you share what is uniquely yours to give.

In the midst of my crisis experience I met a new friend named Fran. She was there for me when I really needed her. Our friendship began when I decided to risk peeling back a part of my mask. Fran, who was a member of the Bible study group that met in my home, was very support-ive and loving. Finally, one evening after the Bible study I said to Fran, "I want to thank you for being so loving to me."

Her response was, "Oh, it's easy."

Encouraged by her answer, I decided to risk being vulnerable to her by saying, "It is? You don't know how unloveable I feel."

Hearing this, Fran didn't try and contradict me. She just said, "Well, I guess you need us to love you right now." Not only was I able to verbalize my feelings to her, but she validated them without judging me. At that point a small seed of trust was planted, and our friendship grew. Fran became a very valued person in my life.

Intimacy develops through the seesaw of trust and risk taking. Every time you peel back your mask and reveal a private hope, feeling, or dream, you're risking that the other person may use the information to hurt you. Once you make yourself vulnerable to another person and you find out that your secrets are safe with them, trust grows. Gradually you become less and less wary about taking risks with that person and an intimate friendship forms.

What Will You Choose?

You have the option of moving and growing beyond your present situation. No matter how distrustful you feel, no matter how hurt you are, you still have choices. You can either live your life in bitterness and in fear of being rejected, or you can choose to make the most of your situation by working through your feelings and learning to take risks again.

Yes, taking a risk involves pain. So does not taking a risk. Taking a risk, however, promises greater rewards than staying in your lonely fortress. Who knows what great plans God still has for your life? You'll never find out until you decide to start trusting again.

I know it's hard. I know because I've been there. I also know that someway, somehow, if you'll allow Him, God will use what you've been through to help someone else. No matter how bleak or drastic the situation is now, God can and will make something positive out of it, if you'll let Him.

My favorite Scripture concerning this is Luke 22:31–32, in which the Lord is talking to Simon Peter: "Simon, Simon! Indeed, Satan has asked for you, that he may sift you as wheat. But I have prayed for you, that your faith should not fail; and when you have returned to Me, *strengthen your brethren*" (emphasis mine).

I can tell you from experience that learning to trust again is worth the risk involved. I know because when my life was in shatters:

- I never felt so worthless.

- I never felt so inadequate.

- I never felt so rejected.

Since that time:

- I have never seen God's love outpoured for me as I have now.

- I have never been a more "real" person than I am now.

- I have never felt more empathy and compassion for hurting women as I do now.

Learning to take the risk again made all the difference in my life. It can make all the difference in your life as well.

INTIMACY:
Building Close Relationships

*Blessed are they who have the gift
of making friends,
for it is one of God's best gifts.
It involves many things, but above all,
the power of going out of one's self
and appreciating whatever is noble
and loving in another.*

—Thomas Hughes[1]

CHAPTER EIGHT

When I lived in Oregon I was only an hour's drive from the gorgeous Oregon coast where I often vacationed. I loved to take long, solitary walks along the wide, sandy beaches. The smell of the salt air, the sand between my toes, and the overwhelming beauty of my surroundings always helped put my problems into perspective. To think that the God who created the oceans also loved and created me!

I've noticed, though, that solitary walks along the beach often have a way of emphasizing loneliness. Even though I enjoy the chance to be alone and hear myself think, I also miss having someone with whom to share the beauty around me. At those times I'm made aware of the basic human need for companionship. Whether it's to share an ocean view, or just to share our daily lives, we all want an intimate relationship with at least one person with whom we can share our thoughts, feelings, and the world around us.

Real intimacy requires a certain level of communication. Although we communicate with people every day, it is usually not on the intimate level we crave. There are several rungs on the communication ladder, and most of the time we find ourselves conversing on one of the lesser rungs. To understand this, look at a brief description of each rung:

Superficiality is the first rung. On this level you communicate with someone through standard conversation such as, "Have a nice day" or "How are you?" On this rung you say what is expected of you. Even if you are having a rotten day, you say you're "fine." This is the lowest rung of the communication ladder because you're not even required to tell the truth.

Storytelling is the second rung of the communication ladder. On this level you share facts and newsworthy information such as, "I read an article in a magazine about making quilts and it said . . ." or "When I traveled to Europe, I learned that . . . ." This is often the conversational method you use with someone you've just met because it doesn't require you to share anything personal.

Sharing sentiments is the third rung. On this level you start to reveal yourself. Sharing your sentiments means stating your opinions or disclosing your ideas. At this point you start to risk peeling back your mask, although on a small scale. If the other person slams the door on your idea or opinion, you can easily move back to one of the first two rungs of the ladder.

Sharing sensations is the fourth rung on the communication ladder. On this level you can share your feelings and emotions. At this point you expose your inner thoughts and hopes, and the other person reciprocates. If you've reached this level with someone, you know how wonderful it feels.

Supreme sharing is the top rung of the ladder. This is the ultimate form of communication because along with sharing your feelings and emotions, you are also able to risk exposing your faults and shortcomings, assured in the knowledge that the other person will still accept you. On this level you can risk revealing your mistakes without fear of judgment. You and the other person share a personal commitment to each other, one that brings complete freedom in communication. We all need and desire this freedom in communication. On this level true intimacy is achieved.

Each rung on the communication ladder serves a purpose, but most of us desire at least one relationship that reaches the supreme sharing level. If this is true, why don't more of us have it? Often we've been misled about the nature of true intimacy. Possibly we've been searching for this intimate form of communication in all the wrong places. Many of us believe these five things about intimacy:

1. Intimacy is with the opposite sex only.
2. You're intimate if you live with someone.
3. You're intimate if you spend a lot of time with someone.
4. You're intimate if you're married to someone.
5. You're intimate if you've had sex with someone.

All of the above statements are false. They are not accurate measures of intimacy. If you've been looking for intimacy through sex, marriage, or quantity time spent with someone, you'll be disappointed. True intimacy doesn't require any of these things. How then can you achieve intimacy? By embarking on a journey in which you'll learn to reach out to others, hold a confidence, be a good listener, and be an encourager.

Reach Out to Others

If you're hurting or feeling lonely, it's your responsibility to let someone know. Since another person cannot read your mind, you've got to take the first step and express how you're feeling.

When I am having a particularly bad day it's important for me to tell the people around me. Otherwise they might think that it's their fault. If I'll just say, "I'm feeling grumpy today. It's not your fault, I'm just feeling stressed," it can make all the difference. By reaching out and letting others know how I'm feeling, I'm keeping the lines of communication open.

We close communication lines with our anger or bitterness. I have a friend, Sally, who is consumed with bitterness because she feels fellow Christians rejected her when she went through a divorce. She has said on more than one occasion, "Everyone deserted me. When I was in the worst pain and needed someone, no one was there." Since I know Sally, I also know that her story could have had a different ending. Sally never *told* anyone that she was hurting or that she needed friends. In her pain she often lashed out at people, driving them away, although it was the last thing she meant to do. Then, when she found herself alone, she was bitter that no one had read her mind or mystically understood that her anger was a mask for her pain.

If you are hurting, you've got to let people know. This doesn't mean that you hold a pity party and invite all your friends, but it does mean that you give people an opportunity to help you.

I often had to force myself to reach out to others. In the midst of my pain and confusion I had to *choose* to get involved in a women's Bible study group. Once I joined, I then had to swallow my pride and admit to the women there that I needed them. At first it wasn't easy, especially since I was used to being the counselor, not the counselee. After all, I was the one who traveled every weekend speaking to women's groups. What would people think if they knew that I was hurting and didn't have all the answers?

The women in my Bible study group came through for me like troopers. I have nothing but gratitude in my heart when I think of them. Although I have since moved to California, they are a big reason why part of my heart is still in Oregon. They helped to heal the wounds in my spirit so that bitterness could not creep in and destroy me, as it did my friend, Sally. And it all started when I was willing to risk sharing my feelings with others.

Possibly, you're ready to tell someone about the pain you're feeling, but you feel isolated. Maybe you feel you don't have anyone you can trust with the information. In my experience one of the most isolated groups of women are pastors' wives who are often pressured to perform on a certain level at the church, are expected to be nearly perfect, without problems, and to be giving to others. If they experience problems with their family or husband, who can they tell? Usually their friendships are based in the church congregation, and for obvious reasons they feel unable to share on a personal level with other church members. What can be done in this situation?

I know of one pastor's wife who was confronted with just such a problem. She couldn't share her innermost feelings and difficulties with women in her congregation, but she didn't throw up her hands and resign herself to isolation. Instead, she decided to instigate her own fellowship group made up of other local pastors' wives. Together these wives formed a bonded group for fellowship and sharing. What a great idea!

When I first moved to California I also felt very isolated. I didn't know anyone in the city of Fremont, where I now live. I had learned enough in my healing process, however, to know that I would have to make the effort to develop friendships. I couldn't just twiddle my thumbs, hoping that someone would miraculously call me up and ask to be my close friend. One of my former Image Improvement teachers, Rita Lamphere, an old and good friend, lived nearby, so I called and asked her to lunch.

The lunch with Rita was a wonderful time of further developing our friendship. Rita was very supportive and loving, and we made a commitment to continue to develop our friendship. As time went by Rita and I grew closer and closer. She proved to be an encouraging, trustworthy, and loving friend.

A few months later, Becky Martin, another former Image Improvement teacher, moved to Fremont, and she began joining us for times of sharing. Together the three of us made a commitment to meet once a month for a whole day of prayer and sharing. We had an agreement that whatever we shared would not be passed along to anyone else, and our trust in each other grew. At a time when I really needed it, I developed two close friendships; all because I decided to risk reaching out to others.

If you're feeling isolated, try to expand your horizons. Make the first move, take the first step, explore all the different avenues that may lead you to a sharing, intimate relationship. Let others know you need them.

Another reason it is important to reach out to others is that you need to be accountable to someone else. If you're grieving over a loss, struggling with an addiction, or just trying to put your life back together, you need to be accountable to someone else for your progress. This person may be your pastor, close friend, professional counselor, or possibly a group of people such as a church Bible study or fellowship group. The important thing is that you meet on a regular basis with at least one person and talk about how you're doing.

The reason for accountability is simple. If you don't have someone with whom to "check in," it is too easy to stagnate and never grow at all. Being accountable to someone means that you're conscious of making improvements in your situation. The idea is to move forward, not slip backward. With help, any backward steps can be corrected. Without help, chances are you'll just keep slipping.

During my crisis experience, I was accountable to the women in my Bible study group. Once a week we met and shared our progress. Knowing I was going to be seeing them each week helped me continue to improve my situation.

If you don't have someone to whom you are accountable, it's up to you to change the situation. Start by checking out the available support groups at your church. Or, make an appointment to talk with your pastor. If your church is small, you may want to call a larger Christ-centered church in your area. Many of the larger churches offer specialized support groups for various problems. Others have small "covenant" groups that meet on a weekly basis. Just make sure that you're accountable to someone so that you'll be encouraged to keep going, growing, and making progress.

Hold a Confidence

As you reach out to others you'll most likely find that they are also reaching out to you. When this happens, and you're making progress toward developing an intimate friendship, it's crucial that you keep a confidence. Nothing will ruin a potential relationship quicker than a loose tongue. If someone has shared inner feelings and problems with you, it's vital that you keep the secrets. This holds true in any sort of friendship, but especially if you want to develop trust and intimacy. The only information you should be revealing to a third party is the type that passes the following criteria:

1. Is it true?
2. Is it kind?
3. Is it necessary to tell?
4. Is it beneficial to all concerned?
5. Do you have the other person's permission to share the story?

Use these five questions as your rule of thumb when you're tempted to divulge someone else's business. If the answer to any or all of these five questions is no, you're just asking for trouble if you pass it along.

It is imperative that you learn to keep a confidence, but to be fair, I must mention one exception to this rule. Breaking a confidence is justified if the people involved have violated the law. If someone confides in you about something criminal, you could be held accountable if the truth comes out. In this case breaking a confidence is the best alternative.

I was faced with this very difficult choice this past year when a twelve-year-old girl at my seminar wrote on her prayer request that her stepfather was "slipping into her room at night." I always assure my seminar attendees that their prayer requests are kept confidential, and up until that point, I had always kept my word. This time, however, I was confronted with a situation that I couldn't repress. Since the girl had signed her full name to the prayer request, I was able to get her telephone number. I phoned the young girl and told her that I was going to have to let someone know what was happening in her life. I told her that the abuse had to stop and I would do whatever I could to help. After talking with her she decided to tell her mother. Her mother then talked with me and I let the mother know that I was calling the Child Protective Services department in their area so that they could get help. As far as I know the girl is now safe and the family is in counseling. Although I hated breaking a young girl's confidence, I know it was the right thing to do. She was crying out to me for help.

Barring criminal involvement, however, breaking a confidence is a major taboo in developing intimate relationships. There are good reasons why the Bible often refers to keeping control of the tongue. In Proverbs 21:23 it says, "Whoever guards his mouth and tongue keeps his soul from troubles."

My friend, Connie, is a pastor's wife and several years ago she confided to a close friend about a minor personal problem that concerned her husband. Once Connie and her husband moved to another state to pastor a new church, her friend decided to pass along Connie's confidential information to a third party—with a few embellishments added to the story! By the time it got back to Connie, after making the rounds of several people, the story was blown completely out of proportion and didn't have much truth left in it. Connie's husband was hurt by it and the relationship between Connie and her friend was damaged. When Connie confronted her friend about spreading the information, her friend said she didn't know why she had done it and she was extremely sorry about it. Unfortunately, it was too late. Although Connie and her husband are continuing with a thriving ministry, she now feels leery about sharing herself with anyone.

Spreading gossip is no way to develop an intimate relationship. Any time you share someone else's story or situation without their permission you're spreading gossip. In almost every case what you pass along about someone else will eventually get back to them. The grapevine works in two directions! Do you want the other person to know what you're saying?

Be a Good Listener

One way to avoid having a loose tongue is to close your mouth. I don't mean to sound flippant, but most of us need to concentrate on being good listeners. Sometimes consciously making sure our mouths are closed is the right place to start. In learning to develop intimate relationships good listening skills are invaluable.

A few years ago I was having dinner with an acquaintance of mine. We hadn't seen each other for quite some time, and as we chatted over dinner she said to me, "So how is your husband doing?" For a moment I froze. I wasn't sure what to tell her. I had assumed she already knew about the divorce. Obviously, she didn't.

Gathering my courage, as I was still in the midst of a painful situation, I began to talk about the tragic events of the past few months, culminating in the recent signing of divorce papers.

"Oh, well, that's too bad," she replied, as she then changed the subject. Several minutes later she asked me, "So what have you been doing the past few months?"

I almost gasped audibly. In a quiet voice I said, "I've been going through the process of a divorce." Seemingly unaware of her insensitivity, my friend kept on chatting. At that point any chance for rewarding communication was lost.

My daughter, Deanna, had a similar experience several years ago, on the day she found out that her then five-year-old daughter, Kimmi, was going to be attending a school for multihandicapped students. Kimmi, adopted from Korea, has cerebral palsy and is also mentally retarded. Although Deanna was aware that Kimmi had special needs, the news that Kimmi would never lead a normal life was hard for her to assimilate. That afternoon she was visiting with a good friend and began to share what Kimmi's teachers had told her. Fighting back the tears, Deanna said, "It's just so hard to let go of my dreams for Kimmi's future. I feel so sad right now."

As Deanna finished speaking her friend was quiet. She literally didn't say *anything*. Then, without even acknowledging that Deanna had spoken, her friend changed the subject and started talking about her own problems. Deanna was stunned. Although they are still friends, a chance for real and intimate closeness disappeared that day.

What caused Deanna's friend to ignore the pain Deanna was feeling? What caused my friend to gloss over the painful information I had shared about my divorce? Were they both so shocked that they didn't know what to say? Or were they so anxious about their next sentence that they couldn't hear what we said? I suppose we'll never know for sure, but I do know that heart-to-heart talks died because these women were unable to listen.

I have to admit that there are times when I've been guilty of poor listening skills, usually when I'm extremely busy and in the middle of trying to meet a deadline. One day Deanna called during my busy time, and I kept right on working while holding the phone to my ear. Suddenly, I was aware of dead silence on the other end of the line.

"I'm sorry. What were you saying?" I said.

"Nothing," she replied. "I guess I must be boring you."

Fortunately, Deanna understood the pressure I was under. I realized, however, that I needed to stop working for the short time that I was on the phone with her.

Listening is a skill that many of us find difficult to master. Being a good listener requires that you concentrate on the other person, not yourself.

Good listeners:

- devote their complete attention to the person talking.

- keep listening even when they disagree with the person talking.

- avoid giving unsolicited advice.

If you're not naturally a good listener, you can become one. Each one of the characteristics of good listening can be learned. While good listeners may be difficult to come by in this self-absorbed age, the reward is worth the effort: good listeners usually have deeper and more satisfying relationships.

Give Your Undivided Attention

Whenever I get the chance to visit with my sister-in-law, Marilyn, I'm always charmed by her wonderful listening

skills. When you talk with Marilyn her body is always leaning slightly toward you, as if she can't wait to hear what
you have to say next. Her face shows understanding and
empathy. She looks right at you, not over your head or out
the window. She asks pertinent questions that show she is
really interested, and she doesn't interrupt in the middle of
your thoughts. Marilyn has always been my model for
good listening skills.

Give someone your undivided attention by making sure
your eye contact and body language communicate your
interest. When someone else is talking, maintain eye contact. This doesn't mean that you stare at them, but it does
mean, for example, that you put your book down, turn the
television off, or stop writing your grocery list. It's just too
hard to concentrate on two things at once. If your eyes are
looking down at your lap, reading the newspaper, or wandering all over the room, the other person will get the un-
spoken message that you're not interested. Also, lean
forward slightly, *toward* the person who is talking. Leaning
back or away from the person indicates that you're wanting some distance between you.

Instead of thinking how you'll respond when the other
person stops speaking, concentrate on what the other person is saying. This way you'll be able to ask intelligent,
meaningful questions that will indicate how well you've
been listening. Asking pertinent questions will also stimulate the conversation and deepen your communication.

Keep Listening Even if You Disagree

One of the truest tests of an intimate relationship is the
ability to disagree and still maintain the relationship.
When you can listen to someone else without interrupting
or arguing, even when you don't agree with what that person is saying, you're well on the way to intimacy.

When Deanna and I have an intimate talk I sometimes
find that I don't agree with her feelings. Since we come

from two different generations, our opinions don't always coincide. Not that either of us is wrong, it's just that we don't see eye to eye. When this happens, my old childhood programming wants to say, "Deanna, you shouldn't feel that way. Snap out of it!" I really have to take a mental step back. I know that imposing my opinions on Deanna will only alienate her, and I'm learning to respect her opinions, even though they may be different from mine.

Too often we have the tendency to shut our ears when we hear something with which we disagree. Sometimes we even exclude that person from our lives. In very rare instances this has happened to me when I've shared with a church leader the fact that I have been divorced.

Sometimes I have felt hurt and rejected, but I try to remember not to do it to someone else. When I disagree with someone I usually try and keep the lines of communication open. *It is not my place in this world to judge.* Only God has the right to judge. When you or I cease communicating with someone because we disagree with that individual, we assume God's job and, confidentially, we just don't have His qualifications!

Sometimes when we judge, we jump to the wrong conclusions, and we end up looking very foolish. There are times when appearances can definitely be deceiving. To illustrate this, let me tell you about an experience that happened to my daughter.

Deanna, and her husband, Dean, have a unique, "rainbow" family. Robby, the oldest, is adopted from India and has beautiful, dark-brown skin and straight black hair. Aron, their birth son, has curly blond hair and blue eyes. Kimmi, adopted from Korea, has deep olive skin and Asian eyes. Jameson, adopted from Illinois, is of Cherokee Indian heritage and has medium-brown skin and black wavy hair. Shaina, adopted from Maryland, is of African-American heritage and has light-brown skin and curly brown hair. The baby, Fallon, their birth daughter, is very fair complected and has reddish-blonde hair. As I said, they have a rainbow family!

You can imagine what it's like when Deanna takes all the kids to the store with her. People tend to stare, not just at all the ethnic groups represented, but at the sheer number of children! While most people make very favorable comments about such a diverse family, there are exceptions. One day, a woman approached Deanna in the store and said, "Are these all your children?"

"Yes," Deanna replied.

"How could you?" the woman continued.

"Well, I just love children. They're all great kids," said Deanna.

The woman then became irate and started an angry tirade. "I just don't understand how you can sleep around like that. Don't you have any moral character? How many different fathers do they have anyway?"

Stunned by this woman's vehemence, Deanna could hardly believe her ears. Obviously, the woman had judged Deanna without bothering to know or understand the situation. Overcoming her momentary shock, Deanna then took great pleasure in letting the woman know that four of her children were adopted. You can imagine how embarrassed the woman was by her blunder. Deanna has been chuckling about it ever since.

When you judge without trying to understand, intimacy is impossible to achieve. Allow yourself the opportunity to really listen to someone else's unique circumstances without judging. Just like the woman in the store who confronted Deanna, you may find out information that will help you to understand the other person, even if you don't agree. Remember, a good listener respects another person's opinion.

Avoid Giving Unsolicited Advice

While working on this book, Deanna and I have had more than our usual share of heart-to-heart talks. Although we've always been close, working together on the material for this book has caused us to examine our relationship more carefully. Just a few weeks ago, while discussing the information for this chapter, I said to her, "I really want to share what I've learned about not giving unsolicited advice. It's so important not to tell someone else what to do."

"Hmmm, that's interesting," Deanna replied. "So why do you still try and fix my problems?"

I didn't realize what I was doing! I'd been working on using all the right communication skills with other people, but somehow hadn't translated them to my relationship with Deanna. Instead of listening to Deanna share her feelings, I naturally wanted to protect and mother her. I told her what she could or should do in each situation, trying to give her a pep talk when what she really wanted was a listening ear. I now realize that I have to downplay my natural instinct to mother her. After all, she's a married woman and the mother of six children! I guess if she really needs my advice, she'll ask for it!

I've learned that unless someone asks for your opinion, it is best to keep your advice to yourself. Usually people can sort out their problems on their own. They just need a chance to voice their concerns aloud to a sympathetic listener.

When someone is sharing with you, remember that words like *should* or *ought* need to stay out of your vocabulary. Saying, "You should do this . . ." will only alienate your friend. Don't try to coax, badger, or cajole a person in crisis to "Get counseling," "Quit smoking," "See a doctor." Although these may be good suggestions, they are not what someone in crisis needs to hear. The best thing you can do is listen without judging. Let the person cry or sound a little crazy without trying to fix the problem. Say things such as, "You mean so much to me and I'm sorry you're hurting," or "I'm behind you on this and I'll always be on your side," rather than giving advice. Better yet, try "I know you're hurting. . . . Let me know if I can help in any way." This lets the other person know you're ready to help or give advice, *if* she wants to ask for it.

The following poem expresses this idea so beautifully:

When I ask you to listen
And you start giving advice,
You have not done what I have asked.
When I ask you to listen
And you begin to tell me why I
shouldn't feel the way I do,
You are trampling on my feelings.

When I ask you to listen
And you feel you have to do something
to solve my problem,
You have failed me,
strange as that may seem.

Listen,
All I asked you to do was listen,
not talk, or do.
Just hear me.

I can do for myself;
I am not helpless . . .
perhaps discouraged or faltering,
But not helpless.

When you do something for me
that I need to do for myself,
You contribute to my fear and weakness.

But, when you accept as fact
that I feel what I feel,
no matter how irrational,
Then I can stop trying to convince you
and get on with understanding
What's behind that irrational feeling.

And, when that's clear,
The answers will be obvious,
And I won't need any advice.[2]

Learning to listen without giving unsolicited advice will make you one of the most sought-after people in the world. But keep in mind good communication is a two-way street. There will be times when you'll need to express yourself. At those times your words of encouragement will be necessary.

Be an Encourager

Along with being a good listener, you also need to be an encourager, one who uses the power of words to help, not harm, someone else.

When you were small you always looked to others to affirm your abilities. When you tied your first shoe, got an A on your math test, or learned how to ride a bike, you looked to someone else to praise your accomplishments. Hearing words of praise from those people, usually your parents, made you feel like a capable person.

Possibly you didn't hear words of praise. How did it make you feel? Unloved? Worthless? Charles McCabe, a newspaper columnist, once wrote a vivid account of his own feeling of unworth.

> I don't know about you, man, but I was brought up to feel unworthy. Maybe worthless. . . . At home I would do this or that or the other thing, or be thought to be doing this, that or the other thing (which was equally bad) and my mother would make her usual statement. It was generally toneless and without emphasis, because it had been repeated so often and because it had the ring of revealed wisdom: "You'll end up in Sing-Sing . . . ."[3]

Somehow Charles McCabe overcame his mother's dire prediction. He learned to be a responsible and contributing member of society, no thanks to the unaffirming childhood he endured. But you can be sure he has an overwhelming need to hear words of praise, even to this day.

We all need to hear words of praise. You may not have heard them in childhood, but you can start to give and receive them today. In developing an intimate relationship words of praise and encouragement are essential, enabling you to see yourself as a capable, valuable person.

If giving praise is difficult for you, start off by giving compliments. Compliments are words of love. A sincere compliment goes to your very soul, your essence.

Recently, I was preparing for a seventeen-day speaking trip in Germany. I was especially nervous because it would be the first time I had ever spoken with an interpreter. The week before I was to leave, my son, Bobby, called me from his home in Holland. After I explained how nervous I was he said to me, "Oh, Mom, I know you'll be great. You're such a good speaker. You're the best!" His enthusiastic compliment made all the difference in my attitude. Although I know he's biased in my favor, his words of love are good to hear!

In our homes words of praise should be heard at least three times as often as words of criticism. People usually hear all about their failures, but their successes are overlooked. My friend, Terri, was determined not to let this happen in her family.

Terri's son, Benjamin, then thirteen, was having trouble with his schoolwork. One day he brought home a D on his report card, the first one he'd ever received. Looking very forlorn, Ben assured his mother he'd try harder next time. Instead of berating him, Terri smiled, hugged, and encouraged Ben by saying, "I'll look forward to next time."

The next semester, Ben brought home his report card and his D grade had now become a C. When Terri saw it she didn't say, "Well, now you can try for a B." Instead, she started jumping up and down, shouting "Hooray! Let's have a party!" That night the family went out to dinner and celebrated Ben's improvement! What a beautiful way to show love and encouragement.

You can also show your love and encouragement by writing and sending thank-you notes. Too often we take people for granted. In our minds we may say, "Well, they already know we had a good time when we visited them. Why write a note?"

Writing thank-you notes is an important way to show someone that you really care. In our society, where everybody is on the fast track and no one seems to have time for anyone else, taking the time to jot a note to someone can have a powerful effect. Several years ago, when I was still personally teaching the Image of Loveliness course, I sent one of my students an encouragement note. After receiving my note this student phoned me and said, "You'll never know what a difference your note made. I was ready to commit suicide this morning. I believed that nobody cared about me. When I received your card in the morning mail I couldn't believe it. Thank you for making the difference between life and death for me." Since that time you can be sure I've never forgotten the importance of sending notes of love and encouragement to others!

Since I really believe in taking the time to jot notes, I often send short postcards to my son, Bobby, in Holland. Usually I write these notes while I'm on an airplane or waiting for my flight at the airport. Frequently I am in a hurry to get the note written, but I feel so good about being able to send off a word or two. Last year, however, my son informed me that although he loved hearing from me, my notes left him feeling he was somewhat second-rate. Frequently my notes started out saying, "I'm in a rush . . ." or "I'm so busy and I just have a minute . . . ." To him, this implied that he was not important enough for me to stop what I was doing to really communicate with him. I'm so glad he told me! I hadn't realized what I was implying, and although it was never what I really felt, I now know better than to use the "I'm in a rush" phrase.

Nobody wants to feel second-rate: we all want first-class

treatment! Part of giving first-class treatment is learning to express words of love, but you must also learn how to receive words of love from others. Remember, a compliment is a word of love and you squelch a word of love when you don't accept it.

How many times have you heard someone say, "You *like* this blouse? I got it at a garage sale . . ." or "What do you mean I look good? I need to lose twenty pounds!" Many of us need to be taught that the correct way to accept a compliment is to say, "Thank you." That's all that's necessary. Just, "Thank you."

It's rude to contradict or insult those who go out of their way to speak well of us. If you want to add something to your "thank you," make sure it's positive. For example, if someone compliments you on your red dress, don't say, "Thank you, but I think it's the wrong color for me." A much better response would be, "Thank you, I wasn't sure about the color, but knowing you like it makes all the difference."

We all love compliments, so why do we sabotage our chances of getting them? When a loved one says, "You look beautiful today," a good response would be, "Thank you, you've made me feel so good. Now I'll think about what you said all day long." Let others know that you care by learning to accept compliments graciously.

You can also be an encourager by using nonverbal language. To share your joy, show your support, or let someone know you understand, say it through your facial expression and touch.

Your smile can be a great encourager. Do you know that we all smile in the same language? Let others know you care by letting your face show it. Most smiles are started by another smile!

Another way to let people know you care is through your touch. Hugs can work wonders! When I arrive at various cities for my speaking engagements, I'm usually met at the airport by the women's ministry director or whoever is in charge of the seminar. Since I've spoken on the phone to this person and I feel like I already know her, I always reach out and give her a hug when we meet. This hug often sets the mood for the whole weekend.

Some people say that they don't like to be touched, but most of those people will never forget it if they're hugged in the right way. A hug is so affirming—it lets you know someone cares. Sometimes, even when we know the appropriate words it's difficult to say them out loud. At such a time hugs can help to bridge the communication gap.

While we may need to be careful about hugging members of the opposite sex (depending on the situation), the main idea is to show your love through affirmative touch. If hugging makes you feel uncomfortable, try giving a squeeze on the arm or patting someone on the back.

Your aim is to develop more loving communication with another person. Don't force someone who is obviously uncomfortable with physical contact. Keep in mind unique feelings and needs and you'll always keep the lines of communication open.

By working on deepening the communication with the people you love, the pain in starting over will be considerably lessened. Rebuilding your life after a crisis experience can be extremely difficult, but developing new or improved relationships can make the future look bright again. By communicating with others on an intimate level you'll find a terrific reward in increased love, cooperation, good feelings, and better relationships. As Dinah Maria Mulock Craik expresses in this poem:

> Oh, the comfort—the inexpressible
> comfort of feeling safe with a person,
> Having neither to weigh thoughts,
> Nor measure words—but pouring them
> All right out—just as they are—

Chaff and grain together—
Certain that a faithful hand will
Take and sift them—
Keep what is worth keeping—
And with the breath of kindness
Blow the rest away.[4]

MOTIVATION:
Continuing
to Grow and Become

*History has demonstrated that
the most notable winners
usually encountered heartbreaking obstacles
before they triumphed.
They won because they refused
to become discouraged by their defeats.*

—B. C. Forbes

CHAPTER NINE

Starting over is a difficult task for anyone who has faced a major life change, and few people know this better than Heidi McMillan. Heidi was diagnosed as having juvenile diabetes when she was eight years old. Although the exact causes of juvenile diabetes are unknown, two other children in Heidi's neighborhood and Heidi's father all came down with the disease within a period of four months. Doctors concluded that a virus must have been the culprit in her case.

From the age of eight Heidi learned to live with daily testing of her blood sugar level and daily insulin shots. A bright and optimistic girl, she adjusted well and describes her grade school and junior high years as normal. Things changed, however, when Heidi entered her freshman year in high school. That year she started experiencing complications which sent her to the hospital frequently. She'd go to school for a week or two and then end up in the hospital for another week or two.

During her sophomore year Heidi was hospitalized twenty-two times. With 180 school days per year, Heidi was lucky to attend approximately 80 of those days during each of her high school years. Yet amazingly, she graduated on time, with a 3.8 grade point average. As she puts it, "The Lord blessed me with a good brain, and I just made the most of it." With only one or two exceptions Heidi completed all of her high school courses without the aid of a tutor. She simply read all the textbooks, borrowed class notes from friends, and attended as many classes as she could in between hospital visits.

After high school Heidi enrolled in her local community college to pursue her interest in drama and theater. This continued for just over a year, when Heidi suffered major medical complications that included a blood clot in her lung.

Heidi almost died. She was hooked up to a respirator and her chances looked grim. Although she eventually was able to breathe on her own, she was kept on medication to help thin her blood so the clot would dissolve. Since she was also receiving large doses of pain-killing medicine, she wasn't immediately alarmed when her vision began to blur. One day, after being in the hospital for over two months, her doctor asked her to look at some of her schoolwork. "I can't read it," she said.

Alarmed, Heidi's doctor began running tests on her eyes. At that time Heidi learned that the blood-thinning medication had a very rare side effect that could cause the eyes to bleed. Although the doctors tried to reverse the situation, after several surgeries she lost her sight completely.

At first she was terrified. The only blind people she'd ever known were the ones she'd seen sitting on the streets asking for money. In her limited experience she didn't know any blind people who were actually contributing members of society. Of course, she knows better now, but at the time she believed her dreams of a happy future were gone.

Not only did Heidi lose her sight, but almost all of her friends. Sadly, her former friends weren't able to adjust to her blindness. She felt abandoned. In her confused state she thought, *If my friends can't even accept me, then I guess God can't use me anymore either.*

Two months after losing her sight, Heidi enrolled at a school for the blind to try to make some sense out of her situation. She hated it. She was feeling discouraged, depressed, and angry. In other words, she was still working through the grief process. Shortly after enrolling in the school, she dropped out.

For the next year she continued to work through the grief process. She began making new friends at church but still didn't know how she'd ever fit into society again. Finally, about a year after going blind, she met a new friend who treated her as a normal, functioning human being. For the first time since her blindness someone included her on hiking outings, invited her to concerts, and told her funny jokes that made her laugh. All at once she realized that she was still the same Heidi with the same outgoing personality. She still loved life and knew that she had a lot to contribute. She said, "Lord, I want to get on with my life, but I can't go any further on my own. I can only live one more day *through You*." At that point, she says, she was able to stop looking behind her at what she'd lost and start looking ahead at what the Lord still had in store for her.

Although Heidi happens to be blind, she also knows that no one passes through life without pain or misfortune. As she says, "A lot of people become obsessed with what went wrong. I focus on how fortunate I am. I lost my sight—but I still have my life."

Heidi is a wonderful example of someone who has discovered the secret to starting over. She has learned to focus on what is left, not what was lost. Everyone, at some point or another, experiences heartbreak. Some people get through it and grow beyond it; others get stuck. Why? In order to work through and grow beyond your present heartache, you must keep looking forward: stop focusing on what is lost, and start focusing on what is left.

Through the years since the crisis experience that shattered my life, I've learned to focus on what I have left. Before my crisis experience I had a career that helped women with their self-image, especially by concentrating on improving the outer appearance. I was well-known as a wardrobe consultant and beauty expert. Now, my focus has changed. While I still endorse women looking good on the outside, I realize that I need to address much more serious issues. As I travel and speak each weekend I talk about the issues of forgiveness, self-worth, and building intimate relationships, based on Scriptural truths. My desire is to reach out to other hurting people with a life-changing message of hope.

In the summer of 1990, I had the privilege of speaking in Germany at a large leadership conference for "Euronet," a European product company owned by Ken and Doris Pitman.[1] This company has thousands of distributors, and I was able to meet many of them.

One of the most memorable events during this conference was meeting two couples who had just come from East Germany. Since the Berlin wall had only been down for a few months, it was the first time these people had experienced a motivational meeting. They were so overwhelmed and excited about the possibility of success in life. I was moved to see that as these couples experienced freedom for the first time, they didn't take anything for granted. Everytime they spoke to the Pitmans, there were tears of gratitude in their eyes. These couples were starting over after age forty, discovering what it was like to dream new dreams and have a future filled with hope.

Along with my East German friends, I've also learned to dream new dreams. I've learned to become more of what God wants me to be. And I'm not done yet! I'm still learning, growing, and anticipating the future. I'll never be able to say, "I've learned all there is to know." Each day that I'm living is an opportunity for new growth. If I fail to grow, then my heartache was in vain. I am responsible for moving forward from here.

Heidi, too, has learned this basic philosophy. Now she is

moving forward with her life and has new goals. One of these goals is to reach out and minister to other hurting individuals. Having accepted her blindness, she began working with junior high and high school kids through a Christian program called Young Life. She also volunteers her time at a nursing home. By sharing what she had learned she helps others who are also struggling to rebuild their lives, and in so doing continues to look ahead, not behind.

In the process of working through your personal heartache, I hope that you will keep looking ahead too. Try not to dwell in the past. Let God begin His new work in you today. Isaiah 43:18–19, says, "Do not remember the former things, nor consider the things of old. Behold, I will do a new thing. . . . I will even make a road in the wilderness and rivers in the desert."

I believe that God wants to chart an original path for your life, one in which there will be new growth and refreshment, even in what seems to be a barren desert. Are you ready to allow God to rebuild your life?

Dream New Dreams

If you are starting over, now is the time to let yourself dream. Let God speak to you and show you His great plans for your life. Now is the time to let your unique talents shine.

As you allow yourself to dream, consider all your options, even if some of them seem farfetched. You may never know what you can accomplish until you try. Almost every advance in science, art, or business has occurred when someone dared to try a new approach.

Beethoven, a musical genius, started losing his hearing while still a young man in his twenties. Although he contemplated suicide at first, he later wrote:

What humiliation if someone near me heard a distant flute, and I heard nothing. If someone heard a shepherd sing, and I still heard nothing. These events led me to despair! I almost took my own life! Only my music could hold me back. I felt it impossible to leave this world before having fulfilled my calling. Only thus did I preserve this wretched life.[2]

Beethoven's dream literally kept him alive. He knew that he still had music in his soul and symphonies that needed to be written. Fortunately for millions of music lovers, he didn't give up. As a deaf man Beethoven broke all the rules about how a symphony should be written. While composing Beethoven would hold an accoustical stick of wood between his teeth and press it against the piano. This way he could grasp some of the musical vibrations released while he played. An acquaintance once said of Beethoven, "His musical sense is such that he can do without his hearing."

Beethoven devised a new approach and demonstrated that there is more than one way to write a symphony! There may also be more than one way to write the symphony of your life. There may be options and possibilities that you haven't yet considered. Many situations in life seem to have only one choice of direction when in reality there are many choices. This was true when my daughter, Deanna, graduated from high school. She felt she had only one option—go to college. Although she had no clear idea what to pursue, she dutifully went to college because it was "the only thing to do."

In hindsight Deanna can see many options for her future that she never allowed herself to consider. Although college was a good choice, there were other good choices. For one, she loved to sing, and she knew about an opportunity to join a Christian singing/drama group that traveled throughout the U.S., giving year-round performances. On the other hand, she could have gotten a job and saved money for her long-dreamed-of trip to Europe. Possibly she could have fulfilled another dream by joining a youth mission organization and working in Africa for a year. All of these options were good, respectable, and interesting. They would have given her the time she needed to decide what she really wanted to do with her life.

How many times do we do something because it is expected of us? How many choices do we make based on what others want of us? We need to realize that at most turning points in our lives, there are usually several right answers.

Take the time to consider the right answers for your situation. Don't settle for the first right answer; look for a second, third, or even tenth. Try asking, "What are *some* answers to this situation?" instead of, "What is *the* answer?" Don't pressure yourself or allow others to pressure you. Expand your possibilities. Give yourself the opportunity to dream.

A few years ago, my friend, Linda, at age forty-five, was a married woman with two grown children. She was happy, had her own flourishing business career, and looked forward to early retirement within ten years. Everything seemed perfect until the day her doctor informed her she was pregnant! Good-bye early retirement, hello diapers.

Linda couldn't believe it. Her mind began a litany of protests: she'd had her tubes tied years ago, she was too old; her children were already grown. She was supposed to become a grandmother, not have a baby herself. This was impossible! Unfortunately, nobody informed the baby. Linda was most definitely pregnant.

When Linda's husband found out, at first he was shocked, then concerned, and ultimately elated. To him, this baby represented a second chance. When his other children were small, he'd been busy making his way in the business world. Now he could relax and devote more time to being a family man.

Linda did not share her husband's enthusiasm. She felt she was facing the end of her business career. Her husband had the very strong opinion that Linda should quit her job and stay home when the new baby arrived. Finances were not a problem, and he believed in full-time motherhood. Although Linda had stayed home when the other children were small, she wasn't sure she could so easily give up everything she'd worked for in her career.

For quite a while Linda believed she had no other choice but to quit her job and devote herself exclusively to motherhood. After all, she had an obligation to her husband and she didn't want to disappoint him. Her options seemed limited. With a new baby on the way her dream of a successful career, topped off by a worry-free, early retirement, was gone. She felt trapped and resentful.

This resentment kept her from dreaming new dreams. She was unable to see any other choices until she read a magazine article about taking the time to evaluate options. As she contemplated her situation she realized that some of her options included: quitting her job until the baby was old enough for school and then resuming her career; beginning a new career that would allow her to be with her child (such as starting a day-care center in her home); or finding a part-time job so she could be at home and still keep working.

Once Linda started to evaluate her options (which were all right answers depending on what she decided), she came upon just the right answer for her situation. Her employer was willing to let her try job sharing. In this situation she'd keep her same job but share the hours and responsibility with another person. Working fewer hours, she'd be able to be home much of the time with her new baby while still maintaining her sense of identity in the business world.

As she explored the idea of job sharing Linda began to dream a new dream. After several discussions with her husband he agreed to the job sharing arrangement, and Linda found her resentment disappearing. She began to look forward to having a new baby and didn't feel trapped into making an unwanted decision.

Although juggling both a career and motherhood is exhausting at times, Linda has found it to be very rewarding. Her daughter, Ashley, is a constant source of joy in her life, and her business career is still going strong.

Instead of feeling trapped, Linda learned the value of evaluating her options and dreaming new dreams, an important step in charting a new path for your life too. Take the time to really look at your situation. Evaluate your options. Eventually, after prayerfully considering all the right answers for your situation, you'll be able to choose the best one for you.

Be Determined

If you allow yourself the opportunity to dream new dreams, the right dream will then become your new goal, but to reach this goal will require commitment. Without determination you may easily become discouraged and give up. With determination your dreams can come true.

Thomas Alva Edison was a determined man. Probably the greatest inventor of all time, he had only three months of formal schooling. But he didn't let this stop him from changing the lives of millions of people through such inventions as the electric light. During his lifetime, he patented more than 1,100 inventions.

Edison defined genius as "1 percent inspiration and 99 percent perspiration." He lived this belief by working days at a time, stopping only for short naps. Edison was nothing if not determined. He rarely stopped working on his inventions until he got them right. Failure never discouraged him. After 10,000 experiments with a storage battery failed to produce the desired results, a friend tried to cheer him up. "Why, I have not failed," Edison said, "I've just found 10,000 ways that won't work."

When Edison's laboratory burned down in 1876, destroying much of his research, he didn't throw in the towel. Instead, he picked up the pieces and started over again. The very next year, he came up with one of the world's most original inventions. No one else had ever made a working model of it, and Edison's design was absolutely new. We call it the phonograph.

I'm inspired by Thomas Edison. He didn't give up after 10,000 failed experiments. He didn't give up when his laboratory burned down. No matter what obstacles he faced, he was determined to keep learning and growing. And every time I turn on a light switch or listen to my record albums, I benefit from his determination.

Heidi McMillan didn't give up either. In the process of starting over she went back to the school for the blind. Even though she had once hated it, she now had a new dream and a new goal. This time she didn't go back as a student, she went as a minister to the other blind students. She knew from talking with them that many of them were feeling lonely, discouraged, and bitter, just as she once had. With her rediscovered optimism and new determination, Heidi shared with these people the joy she had found in trusting the Lord. The other students often told her that they couldn't believe she was blind and also joyful. Heidi touched many people's lives and soon started a Bible study. Before long, many of them were also experiencing new growth and new dreams.

Last year Heidi got married. She met her husband, Randy, three years ago, when he spoke to a group at her church. Randy, an accomplished pianist, was also a local media personality—a sports announcer on the radio. As Randy shared his testimony, played the piano, and talked about different sporting events, Heidi was intrigued. Here was someone who was contributing to society and making an impact. Here was someone who also had a dream to minister to others. Here was someone who, like Heidi, was blind.

Together, Heidi and Randy McMillan have now formed an organization appropriately called, "Out of Sight Ministries." Their desire is to reach discouraged, disheartened people who need to dream new dreams. The theme verse for their ministry is Luke 4:18 which says in part, "He has sent Me to heal the brokenhearted, to preach deliverance to the captives and recovery of sight to the blind."

Since she became blind almost five years ago, Heidi has had several other surgeries and hospital stays because of insulin complications. Although others would view these episodes as setbacks, Heidi sees them as opportunities for new growth and remains joyful, enthusiastic, and optimistic about her future. She is determined to carry out the dream God has planted in her heart.

Heidi was helped in her determination by her husband and a loyal group of friends from church. They became her accountability group. Whenever she felt discouraged, they never let her say, "I can't." In fact, they made sure she stuck with her *can't,* until she *could.*

In rebuilding your life, determination is one of your greatest assets. To stay determined stick with your *can't* until it becomes a *could.* Don't get bogged down with "impossibilities." At one time, cars, airplanes, microwave ovens, and computers were all impossibilities. Even celebrating Christmas was an impossibility until God made it possible. Your own impossibilities are definitely possible. With God's help and your determination your dreams *can* become a reality.

James C. Corbett was a champion prize-fighter of an earlier era. In writing on the subject of determination he said, "When your feet are so tired that you can hardly shuffle back to the center of the ring, fight one more round. When your arms are so tired that you can hardly lift your guard, fight one more round. When you wish your opponent would put you to sleep, fight one more round. The man who fights one more round is never whipped."[3]

If you're not naturally a determined person, here are some things that will help keep you motivated:

- Look for an inspirational role model.

- Find a new hobby.

- Look for the humor in your situation.

All of these things can help to keep your spirits up, so that even if you face obstacles, you won't be tempted to quit.

Look for a Role Model

One of the best ways to keep yourself motivated is to look for an inspirational role model. Knowing or reading about people who, despite major obstacles, have made a success out of their lives, can be just the encouragement you need to keep yourself growing and moving forward.

Heidi McMillan is an inspiration to me, and I've known other inspirational people as well. One of them is Amber Stime. Amber, who was born in Ethiopia, has a life story that demonstrates just how God's unique plan can unfold.

For Amber, God truly charted a new path in the wilderness. Tragedy has been turned into the starting point for opportunity. Amber's parents were Ethiopian farmers who raised their crops on a small plot of land. As with most Ethiopian farmers they still cultivated their crops in much the same way as their ancestors.

A developing country, Ethiopia has also been a land of many wars and border skirmishes, and these battles have taken their toll in more ways than one. When Amber was two years old, her family was visiting a neighbor's farm. While there, Amber and the neighbor boy toddled out to play in the surrounding fields. Before long they discovered a deadly "toy"—an explosive mine left over from a previous war. Not realizing the danger, Amber and the neighbor boy began playing "hot potato" with it. Tragically, it exploded, and Amber lost both of her hands and part of her arms below the elbow. The neighbor boy got shrapnel in his eyes and was blinded.

Immediately following the accident, Amber's parents took her to a Norwegian mission hospital located in the nearest city, some miles away. Having no other resources, they sold their goats to pay for her medical expenses. At the hospital the doctors stitched Amber back together as best they could.

Since Ethiopia is a developing country, advanced medical procedures are generally not available, and Amber's father was advised to have Amber put to death since she would be unable to work and contribute to the family after the loss of her hands. The prevailing wisdom was that death was a better alternative than a "useless" life.

Amber's father could not bring himself to have his daughter put to death. Instead, he took Amber to the capital city of Addis Ababa. There, Amber had an influential relative, an uncle who would be able to help. Amber's uncle was one of Emperor Haile Selassie's priests, and eventually he became the high priest for the Ethiopian Christian Church, the official church of the land. Since her uncle had powerful connections, her parents believed that he would be able to get Amber the help she needed.

Amber lived for the next two years with her uncle in a home that adjoined the emperor's palace. Knowing the limited resources available in Ethiopia at the time, Amber's uncle finally persuaded her father to let Amber live in the British-run orphanage where she would have access to more advanced medical help. Amber lived at the orphanage for the next four years, receiving good care from the missionaries.

During this time the Stimes, a missionary couple, came

to work at the orphanage for one year. After they returned to America, they decided to adopt one of the children, but they couldn't decide which one.

A member of Emperor Haile Selassie's court, a volunteer at the orphanage, heard about the Stimes's interest in adoption and recommended that they adopt Amber, even offering to help with the expenses. In 1970, at the age of eight, Amber arrived in the United States as the Stimes's new daughter. After living with the Stimes for about four months, Amber went to the Shriner's hospital in Minnesota, where she was fitted with prosthetic devices, artificial limbs.

As she was growing up Amber's parents instilled in her a sense of independence and the belief that she was capable of accomplishing anything she decided to do. Although Amber jokingly says she's a "triple minority"—being African-American, a woman, and disabled—she hasn't let that stop her. Now, Amber drives a car, enjoys drawing, painting, and even waterskiing! Her so-called disability hasn't limited her potential. Recently graduated with a master's degree in social work, Amber is working at an adoption agency, helping to place other children with special needs.

Children can also be great encouragers. Spending time with my grandchildren always lifts my spirits. My grandson, Robby, who was born in Calcutta, India, has made me realize that I've been so fortunate in so many ways. Compared to what Robby faced as a small child separated from his birth parents, my life has been blessed.

Living in Calcutta's jails, where lost or neglected children are housed, Robby's obstacles included no shoes or coat in the winter, constant hunger, and frequent beatings by his "jailers." You'd expect that Robby would nurse bitterness for the rough treatment he received, but amazingly, he doesn't. With the resiliency of a child Robby has chosen not to dwell in the past. In his new home his eyes sparkle and he laughs easily. He has an attitude of wonder and enthusiasm that is very contagious. If you meet Robby, you'll be won over by his infectious grin and his obvious love for life.

Robby, like other children, has the gift of living in the present, a lesson most adults should learn. Today is all we have. Yesterday may have been a disaster, but yesterday is gone. It's time to make the most of today.

Find a New Hobby

Sometimes we feel discouraged and want to quit because we don't have anything new or exciting happening in our lives. To remedy this, you may need to make your own excitement by developing a new hobby. It doesn't have to be something you plan to do for the rest of your life, just something to stimulate and motivate you, even temporarily.

During my crisis experience, I began taking oil painting lessons. Although I have always loved to draw and paint, I hadn't picked up a paintbrush in over twenty years. Now, even though my attempts are amateur, I have the personal fun and satisfaction of seeing my work hanging on the walls of my home.

Oil painting helped me to use my time creatively, and also heightened my sense of self-esteem. By expressing myself through my artwork I encouraged a sense of capability and accomplishment.

I know of another woman who also used her artistic talents to bring about positive growth in her life. Here's what she wrote to me a few years ago:

> I have thought about you often through the years and wanted to express thanks for the Image of Loveliness course that I took several years ago.

> I did not become skinny, willowy, or gorgeous, but the positive side did stay with me. During your course

you talked about ways to cure discouragement. One of your examples was to bake someone a chocolate pie, or do something for someone else that would give your own spirit a lift. You were right.

A couple of years after taking the course, I went through a divorce. My first Thanksgiving without a family, I wasn't sure I could handle it, because the holidays were so big for me through the years. As an artist, I called my local hospital and went down and sketched "wounded" kids in the hospital. I then left the sketches so the children could give them to their parents. Furthermore, the following year when I was in Brazil, I did the same thing, only there I also had to do the nurses!

I never sign my name to the sketches, so no one knows I do it. I still have permission from the hospital to slip in and out on holiday mornings so that the children will then have a present for their parents. It gives me good tingles for having done something that took very little effort on my part, and in turn creates a good vibration which hopefully keeps going.

This woman has learned to use her talents as a hobby to help encourage other people, and in the process she keeps herself motivated and encouraged. When you're trying to stay motivated for positive change, this is the best type of hobby to pursue—use your talents to help someone else.

You may also find that your hobby will become a part of your new goal or dream, or perhaps even a whole new career, as it did for Debbie Fields.

Just a few years ago Debbie was a young homemaker who enjoyed baking. Her family and friends raved about her chocolate chip cookies, so she eventually tried selling them to local restaurants. Before long her cookies became very popular and she formed a company to market and sell them. We now know her company as Mrs. Field's Cookies, a multimillion dollar business with stores throughout the United States.

Another woman, Margaret Mitchell, started writing a book as a way to pass the time. Forced by an injury to give up her job as a reporter, she began her first and only novel. After nine years of work her book, *Gone with the Wind*, was published.

Still another example of a hobby that takes on a life of its own happened in Betty Graham's life. Betty, a Texas secretary, was also an amateur artist. One day while mixing some new acrylic paints, she came up with something quite different. She experimented and found that it covered typewriting errors. We now know it as Liquid Paper.

Perhaps your hobby will take on a life of its own, but most often it will just add zest to your life and help to keep you motivated. That's what happened in Ardath Evitt's life. She holds the record as the oldest woman ever to parachute. At seventy-four years old she jumped from a small plane, 3,000 feet over Mooresville, Indiana. Her landing was perfect. As she said, "I think anyone, even as old as I am, who can walk and talk and act foolish, might as well have fun."[4]

Which is good advice for finding a new hobby or staying motivated as you rebuild your life—have fun!

Look for the Humor in Your Situation

As you continue to grow and become all that God has planned for you, take the time to find the humor in your situation. You can't be discouraged with a smile on your face. Learning to laugh at your circumstances, or even at yourself, can work wonders in keeping your spirits high. Laughter is very healing and can help put your problems into perspective.

Laughter is an acceptable way to purge emotions. In many instances, laughter and grieving are closely related. If you've ever laughed until you cried, you know what I mean. Being able to laugh at a difficult situation can also provide the emotional distance you need to start serious problem solving.

There have been many times in my life when I've benefited from learning to laugh at myself or at my situation. One such time occurred a few years ago in Bedford, Indiana, then a town with a population of about 14,000 people. I traveled to Bedford to give a seminar, and the townspeople had a special ceremony in my honor. The mayor officially welcomed me to Bedford and presented me with a key to the city—a key about eighteen inches long and made out of native Bedford rock. As the mayor handed it to me, I didn't realize how heavy it was. In front of about 500 people I dropped the key, which broke in two pieces.

I was so embarrassed I wanted to crawl under the platform. Everyone in the audience was silent, and I was waiting for them to "boo" me off the stage. Quietly, someone began to chuckle, and pretty soon the whole audience was laughing. As I heard the laughter I knew I would be all right. I smiled, chuckled a little myself, and apologized to the crowd for my clumsiness. I also promised them that I would have the key repaired and keep it in a special place of honor in my home.

I kept my promise and the key is now glued back together and has a prominent spot in my home office. I love looking at it because it reminds me of a very unique day. Not only was I given a special honor, but laughter saved the day. It's an important lesson for me to learn.

By finding the humor in my situation I'm able to cheer myself up. One of the ways I do this is by playing a "remember when" game. Usually I call up a good friend or get together with my daughter, Deanna, and we reminisce about past funny events. We giggle about the day I dropped the Bedford rock key, and other humorous events, and before long I'm roaring with laughter.

My friend, Heidi McMillan, also used humor to help improve her situation. After going blind and coming to terms with the fact, Heidi invited twelve of her new friends over for a traditional spaghetti dinner, complete with green salad and french bread. She made the dinner all by herself, cleaned the house, and had the table set perfectly.

When Heidi's friends arrived she handed each of them a blindfold. For the entire meal she wanted them to experience what it was like to be blind! Only one of her friends escaped being blindfolded so that he could take pictures and also "police" the other guests to make sure that no one cheated by removing the blindfold.

According to Heidi, the results were hilarious. Her blindfolded guests had quite a time figuring out how to pour the dressing on their salad and eat their spaghetti without making a mess! Some of them even had trouble identifying if they were drinking cola or 7-Up. Heidi had a great time laughing with them! All in all, it was a fun-filled learning experience, one that was good for Heidi, as well as her friends, because she learned to find the humor and make the most out of her situation.

When you look for the humor in your situation, try watching a funny movie, playing a silly game with your family, or reading an amusing book, anything to help stimulate your funny bone. Old photograph albums can also generate a lot of laughter. Somehow the dated hairstyles and clothing bring out the giggles. Use whatever works for you. The idea is to use laughter to keep your attitude positive. That way you'll stay motivated so you can keep growing and becoming all that God intends for you.

Checking in on Yourself

If you find the humor in your situation, look for a new hobby, and find a positive role model, you will have more determination to work toward your goal. However, you may need to occasionally check in on yourself. The following checklist will help you to keep growing in the right direction.

1. Develop your interests. Do what you like to do.

2. Set a goal to make your dreams a reality. Take a class, or read an informational book.

3. Accept the things you cannot change about your life, but change the things you can.

4. Avoid self-pity.

5. Discipline yourself to do the things you *need* to do, not just the things you want to do at the moment.

6. Make a list of the good things you've accomplished in your life. Pat yourself on the back for your accomplishments.

7. Take time for others. Give of your time and energy unselfishly.

8. Don't give up!

If you use the suggestions on this checklist, you'll find that your life will be a place for new growth. The past will no longer interfere with your promising future. You'll find, just as I did, that there is always hope, even in a seemingly hopeless situation.

New Light in the Darkness

If you'll let Him, God will bring new light to your life. To illustrate this point, I once heard a fictional story about a woman whose husband died. On his tombstone she had inscribed, "The light of my life has gone out." A few years later she met and married another man. "I've got to change that tombstone," she said to her pastor.

"No," he said, "just add to it, 'I struck another match.'"

If the light has gone out in your life, it's time to strike another match. The beautiful thing about starting over is that you don't have to stay in the darkness forever. With God's help you can strike another match, light the candles again, and keep moving forward in new light.

As I come to the close of this book I want to share about the new light I've found for each one of the devastating explosions that shattered my life. During the year after my divorce was final, I thought I'd live the rest of my life alone. I didn't want to risk being hurt again. I desperately wanted to erase the pain the divorce caused for myself, my children, extended family, friends, and even my former husband. It took a while for the Lord to bring healing into my life, but eventually I found myself ready to trust again.

Around this time an old friend, Bob Lovelace, came to town. He was also single and asked me out for a date. It was the first time I'd been asked out since I was a teenager! At the time my twin sister and her husband were living with me, so the four of us went out to dinner at a local restaurant. What fun we had!

As Bob and I continued to see each other my self-esteem improved—I felt worthwhile and valuable again. Feelings of trust and love were returning to my heart. It was so wonderful to once again be loved and accepted. Nearly two years after my divorce was final, Bob and I were married.

Although my new marriage has brought much happiness into my life, and also a new intimacy I've never known before, I know that remarriage is not always God's answer after a divorce and it does not compensate for the pain. If you are facing difficulties in your marriage relationship, finding a new partner is not the solution. If at all possible, God wants to restore your marriage. If this is not possible in your situation, however, it may be time to move forward. Through Christ, you can find new healing for your life.

One evening, about a year after my remarriage, my new husband happened to mention my former husband's name. Suddenly, for no reason tears came to my eyes and I began to weep uncontrollably. Tenderly, my new husband put his arms around me and said, "It's okay. You just cry as long and as hard as you want to. We'll work through this thing together."

This is a perfect illustration of what Christ wants to do for you. When you go through painful and difficult times, He wants to tenderly put His arms around you and say, "It's okay. Just cry as long and as hard as you want to. We'll work through this thing together."

In my own life the Lord has tenderly shown me His compassion. I now have a future filled with hope. Through my divorce experience I've gained a new understanding and empathy for other hurting people. The Lord has blessed my speaking ministry and my heart is filled with gratitude that He chooses to still work through me.

I've also found healing in the situation with the woman filing a lawsuit against my company. Many Christian warriors were praying for months about this lawsuit. My lawyers kept offering to settle out of court for a reduced amount, but lawyers for the other side seemed determined to take it to court. With attorney fees and a court battle looming on the horizon I knew I needed a miracle. Fortunately, God is still performing miracles. Out of the blue, my lawyer called and told me that the other side had agreed to a settlement. The actual amount that I had to pay was lower than any of the previous offers that had been rejected. It was wonderful!

The Lord also worked so beautifully in the situation where my company owed unexpected back taxes. In this situation, when the audit was complete, I owed less than the IRS had originally figured. Although I had to sell real estate holdings and cash in my retirement fund, I was able to clear all debts. Once again, after months of heartaches and headaches, the Lord provided that my business would not have to file bankruptcy.

I've also experienced God's healing power in my physical body. After injuring my ankle the doctors told me that I might never have full use of my leg again, and for many months I had to use crutches. At the time it was a possibility that I would always walk with a slight limp. After months of prayer, hard work, and physical therapy, that possibility did not come true. Today my ankle has healed completely.

Through my crisis experience I've learned that God is always there ready to provide a new beginning. Since I've seen His plan unfold in my life, I know that He is able to chart a new path for your life too. He cares about your pain and wants to comfort you. He wants to restore your life, but He can't do it without your help. Do you want to stay in the darkness or move forward in new light? Only you can "strike another match."

I hope that you will choose to rebuild your life, because God has great plans for you. Don't settle for the darkness. Don't settle for anything less than God's best. To remind me of this, I have a paperweight on my desk which is inscribed with this motto: "I will accept nothing less than God's best in exchange for this day of my life!" As I am learning daily you can always start over!

The following appendix was a help to me when I was going through my divorce. I want to share it with you, as I believe the points mentioned here could apply to many situations that involve human failure and the need to start over. In fact, it could easily have been titled, "Hate Sin, But LOVE The Sinner."

Hate Divorce,
but LOVE the Divorced

By Tom Vermillion

The Restoration Principle

Toward the end of Paul's passionate defense of grace he writes, "Brothers, if someone is caught in a sin, you who are spiritual should restore him gently. But watch yourself, or you may also be tempted. Carry each other's burdens, and in this way you will fulfill the law of Christ" (Gal. 6:1–2 NIV).

Who are "the spiritual"? Most of us feel like the "spiritual" are folks who see things just like we do. But in this context "you who are spiritual" speaks of those with a special kind of maturity—a maturity that no longer seeks the things of the world or reasons as the world reasons. It points to those special people whose hearts are immersed with concern about the souls and lives of others. It speaks of an individual who feels no need to sit in judgment, who is gentle in his ways, and who has learned to love as God loves.

The word *restore* in this text is a present imperative verb meaning "to get it together" or "unite completely." It's a word comfortable in houses of healing, not in courts of law. If we understand, it must be seen as a process, not an event, through which broken brothers and sisters are slowly restored to a relationship with the Lord and His body. This notion of restoration referred to in the covenant of grace is like watching a master craftsman restore a once-splendid piece of furniture now cast away by humanity. The craftsman is given to searching out and finding long-discarded pieces—broken, scarred, and battered. He finds a piece saddened and worn from neglect. It's a piece counted worthless and hopeless and unworthy of love or admiration. But he takes it gently in his hand to apply his love and understanding to that piece of wood. He begins to fill in the scars, to remove the cuts, and to smooth rough edges. He strengthens each part of the whole where it is broken or weakened. Sometimes he applies the chisel, sometimes he simply waits. Finally, the piece is restored. Once again it's functional—even beautiful. But this time it has something wrought only by time and scars and gentle renewal—it has character to add to beauty.

If you'll allow some license with the text, Paul is saying, "You who are spiritually mature, you who have been hurt yourselves, you who have laid aside the judge's mallet—seek out the broken and the battered by sin and restore them to wholeness." It may be that the devastated life comes from the consequences of their own sins or they may be victims of another's sins. Paul really doesn't differentiate, he only calls to restore.

He says to the spiritual, "You make them strong again. You give their life beauty once more. You fill in the scars and cover up the hurt. Do it gently with love, care, and concern. Don't try to coerce or force it or short-cut it. It might break and this time be beyond healing."

It is important to know that restoration is an ongoing process. It is not a one-act play performed one night in front of a crowd, but life being mended in a way that takes weeks, months, and even years.

Hate Divorce

The church today faces a dilemma. Our society and our families are dissolving. Marriages and relationships all around us are failing. We're devastated by the reality that even Christian couples are drifting apart and divorcing. And we're perplexed. In the past we really didn't face a dilemma. Divorce was out there, and we were in here. Divorce happened to people we didn't know well . . . unbelievers . . . those who "didn't love the Lord." Today it's different. People we know, people who love the Lord, are seeing their lives and families torn apart by divorce. It's no longer an insignificant number, and we no longer have the luxury of pretending the issue doesn't exist for the church.

How do we respond to the dilemma? How do we juggle the call of restoring those broken by sin and at the same time maintain the integrity of Scripture that denounces divorce?

When we think about divorce, it's clear that God hates it (see Mal. 2:16). But it is also true that the divorced hate divorce. In fact, God is divorced. In Jeremiah 3:16 (NIV), the Lord says through the prophet, "Have you seen what faithless Israel has done? She has gone up on every high hill and under every spreading tree and has committed adultery there. I thought that after she had done all this she would return to me but she did not. . . . I gave faithless Israel her certificate of divorce and sent her away." God divorced Israel. It's a little staggering to think of God as divorced—but there it is.

Could it be that God hates divorce not so much because of the "terrible people involved in divorce" but because of the terrible pain it brings into the lives of those who experience it? Yes, it is sin. Yes, covenants are broken, unfaithfulness occurs, and selfishness drives apart those who once loved. But could it be that part of the real issue with the Lord is that He personally experienced that pain of divorce, the loss of His bride Israel whom He loved and held so dear? God felt pain, the loneliness, and the rejection from the one He loved. He hurt and longed for His bride to return but she would not.

God hates divorce. It's a deep hatred. But it's not because people involved are always evil, don't love the Lord, have no conscience, or don't honor their contracts. Rather it is because divorce devastates and creates so much hurt and deep pain in the lives of parents, children, husbands and wives. Anything that brings that much pain into life God must hate.

Well, then, how do we respond to divorce? God hates it, so we must hate it. Not because of the people involved but because of the pain involved. The church must always hate divorce, but love the divorced. Somehow we must learn to separate the action from the actor. We must learn to look past the stained veneer to that part of the person that can be restored to beauty, wholeness, and fruitful service to God.

The church today is called to oppose, actively resist, and teach against divorce. We oppose divorce because of the pain it inflicts on everyone it touches. In those relationships where divorce looms on the horizon, where problems are evident and couples are drifting apart, we need to be there and be involved. We need to be calling our people to surrender their will to God. The church needs to be in the business of encouraging and strengthening marriages. We ought to be there with counsel and prayer and support for the family. We should oppose divorce and beat it at every turn.

That's all well and good. It's easy to agree on that aspect of our response to divorce, but there is another question, a tougher one. After all these things have been done by the church—after we have preached against divorce, prayed for the couple, provided marriage counseling, involved the elders in hours of visiting and encouragement—after all this and the divorce still occurs, then what? How do we respond to the divorced? How do we respond when the divorce was not "for fornication?" What do we say to a world of single-again Christians who have been away from the Lord but who now want to return and start their lives over again?

Responding Like Jesus

How would Jesus respond to a brother or sister whose marriage had died? What would the Lamb of God do? What do you picture in your mind as that hurting individual comes to Jesus—divorced, yet wanting to love again, to belong again, to serve again? Can you really see Him cross-examining the defendant, trying to ruthlessly determine the "scripturality of the divorce"; sorting out "guilty" and "innocent parties" so penalties could be levied? Can you see Him turning and walking away without a word? Or do you see Him standing up on His toes, pointing a finger and declaring, "You've made your bed, now sleep in it?" Perhaps you see Him quoting Scriptures about the sin of divorce or making sure this person knows how angry God is about divorce. Do you see Jesus casting him/her out of the synagogue where he/she has come fearfully seeking help?

I hope you can't even imagine Jesus responding in those ways. The Scriptures reveal God in Jesus as one who would be holding that person in His arms with a tear in His eye, feeling the pain they are feeling and asking them to accept the Father's love and forgiveness. I think He would be speaking of life renewed by Him rather than the past marred by sin. It's there that we need to see the church not shutting people out, not casting people off, not sitting in judgment, not preaching self-righteously after the fact; but holding, comforting, healing, and giving hope. As the priests of God we are to embrace them—feel the pain they feel and begin the gentle process of restoration. The church certainly has a prophetic role of declaring God's Word and His judgments. But it also has a priestly function of extending God's forgiveness and healing in redemptive moves. It seems to me that our role is to live lives that are redemptive in nature and to do those things in each case that have redemptive effect.

In this issue of divorce, whatever we do in the Spirit of Christ will be redemptive. We must reach out and touch those who have failed to match God's ideal marriage, who are bearing guilt of their own condemnation and experiencing the pain and rejection of life. Our task is to draw them closer to the Lord and restore them gently. Sometimes we have to force ourselves to look past our doctrinal stances and see Jesus, see Him at the well with a Samaritan woman, a divorcee, a cohabitor. He speaks with the woman, not at her or about her. He speaks of life and hope and living water. He speaks of the future and gently points her to the Savior. He could have scolded. He could have told her how terrible she was and how God could have nothing to do with her because of her life-style. He could have rehashed all of her past sins and marriages and chastised her for living with her boyfriend now. But that wouldn't have been the redemptive thing. She already understood that those things were wrong. She already lived with a sense of guilt and alienation. She already felt that God had washed His hands of her. What she needed was not more guilt, more condemnation, or more rejection. What she needed was a gentle hand to draw her close and to speak of God's love. The result was powerful. She brought a city to Christ.

Remember the woman taken in adultery, caught in the very act, condemned by the Law, a practicing sinner? There were those present ready to preach, ready to quote chapter and verse, ready to decide the fate of the woman "according to righteousness." But what was the redemptive response? Where was Jesus in all this? There He was drawing in the dirt and finally saying to the woman, "Neither do I condemn you." Here was a woman seeking love and compassion in all the wrong places. Jesus simply showed her where to find it in a way that heals rather than hurts. Ask Zacchaeus, Mary Magdalene, or the publicans and sinners who flocked around Jesus what they needed to draw them to the Lord. Do our own brothers and sisters whose lives are scarred by divorce need less?

No matter what our theology of marriage, divorce, and remarriage, surely we have to agree that we must always act in the most redemptive ways in our encounters with the divorced (or any other person).

Without exception, I think the greatest single issue in the life of divorced individuals is that they want to be loved. That's not much different from the rest of us, but they have a very heightened need for love, acceptance, and approval. After all, they've just been rejected in a very final and overwhelming way by the one person who (once upon a time) meant the most to them in all the world. Suddenly they have been told in a very powerful, emphatic way that "You're not wanted, not loveable, not desirable, not attractive, unworthy, useless." At that point in life the divorced is full of self-doubt. They often are guilt-ridden and wonder if the former spouse was right about them. They're asking, "Am I really a person that someone could love some day? Am I still desirable, attractive? Am I the kind of person that anyone would want to be with?" They envision themselves being sixty years old and totally alone, and that scares them. Their confidence in life and themselves has been shattered. They're not even sure about God at this point. They are not only left by a spouse, but if the church rejects them, who do they turn to for healing and love? They are just alone. Maybe they're afraid the Lord has rejected them because the church has.

In view of all this, how should the church respond to the divorced? Reject them? Draw away or set up barriers? Should we place sanctions on them and make them second-class citizens in the kingdom? What would Jesus have us do?

It is difficult to know how to respond to divorced Christians if you haven't been where they are. Sometimes we mean well but don't do very well. Sometimes we want to help, we want to show love, but we don't know how. We tend to stand off and not reach out because we don't know what to do or say. Our theology makes us uncomfortable, and our inexperience causes us to feel inadequate; so we stay back, and the divorced feel rejected, unloved, and unwanted.

Love One Another

There are some practical things the church can be doing. Jesus said, "By this shall all men know that you are my disciples when you have love one for another." Our task is to love the divorced. We may hate divorce, but we must love those whose lives have been touched by it.

In 1 Corinthians 13, Paul gives us that measuring stick for all our responses; it can be quite helpful here. Paul says, "Love is patient." We need to be patient with those who have experienced divorce. Healing does not often come soon. Give them time to heal. Experts say that on the average it takes about two years for life to be on an even keel again after divorce. It is devastating, so give the brother or sister time. Let them be angry and confused. Accept them even though they make mistakes in judgment. You won't understand why they can't let go of the past or forgive. You'll be frustrated when the individual won't act on your advice. There is so much pain and he/she is operating on such an emotional level that for a while there will not be a lot of clear thinking. Be patient and give them time to move through a healing process at their own pace.

Paul says, "Love is kind." Be gentle, be tactful with that brother or sister going through a divorce. His/her emotions are floating on the surface and are very tender. Remember it was said of Jesus that "a broken reed he will not bruise." That is gentleness toward the broken. Don't try to punish in the name of righteousness or place blame. Don't ignore him/her to let them know how much you think God disapproves of them. God will place the blame if necessary. God will be the judge. It is impossible for us to know what a person has been through or how hard they struggled before divorce occurred. Only the Father knows that.

"Love does not boast." Sometimes we feel self-righteous about our own marriages in the presence of those whose marriages have failed. Sometimes we fail to recognize single-parent families as families. When we have family emphasis week, there is nothing for them and they feel it sharply. Be sensitive to those whose marriages dissolved.

"Love is not self-seeking." Those who are in the process of divorce are extremely fragile and vulnerable. They can be used. In the early days after divorce individuals feel uncertain about their abilities to cope or make decisions. They can be almost desperate for love and approval. Sometimes we want to be in control and make them dependent on us. Sometimes we feel fulfilled by making decisions for them. That's not love. That is meeting our own needs, not theirs. We need to be supportive but not controlling.

"Love is not easily angered." Sometimes we're hurt by someone else's divorce. Sometimes we feel loss and betrayal because someone we love has been hurt or has gone away. Don't take your pain out on the divorced. We don't need to unload our hurt and frustration on them; they're hurting too. Don't try to place the blame. Don't try to figure out who is "innocent" and who is "guilty" to unload your indignation on them. God knows. If repayment is due, it should come from Him. We are called to restore both parties in the spirit of gentleness. It's not always easy. Typically, we don't know what to say. We're threatened, caught up in the notion that if I love and accept the divorced, then I condone divorce. It helps if we remember that God loved us while we were yet sinners—yet He doesn't condone sin. Jesus loved the woman at the well and refused to condemn the woman taken in adultery; but certainly no one suspected He approved of their sins. We can support our divorced Christians in rebuilding their lives, we can avoid sitting in judgment on the couple, we can love and accept and heal the hurt with enthusiasm and never have to feel we are saying divorce is okay.

Let's face it. We may never fully understand all the passages about divorce and remarriage in Scripture. Our best scholars may never agree. We may never feel that we have answered all the questions. But the one thing we can all do, and are compelled to do, is "restore such a one in the spirit of gentleness. Bear one another's burdens and thus fulfill the law of Christ." Certainly, we may err in our understanding of and response to the divorce dilemma, but if I understand the words and heart of Jesus, I would rather err on the side of love and mercy than on the side of "law and judgment." Let's set our hearts and minds to the task always at hand—loving and redeeming those whose lives are torn by sin.[1]

Notes

CHAPTER TWO

1. Fred and Florence Littauer, *Freeing Your Mind from Memories that Bind,* (San Bernardino, CA: Here's Life Publishers, 1988).

2. Donna Hartley, Modesto, CA

3. Letter to Fanny McCullough, December 23, 1862, *Lincoln: His Words and His World,* (Waukesha, WI: Country Beautiful Foundation, Inc. 1965), 66.

CHAPTER THREE

1. Charles R. Swindoll, *Starting Over,* (Portland, OR: Multnomah Press, 1977), 14.

2. Gordon McMinn, Ph.D., Beaverton Family Counseling Center newsletter, (Portland, OR: Winter 1985/86).

CHAPTER FOUR

1. Stormie Omartian, "The Freedom of Forgiveness," Virtue magazine, (Sisters, OR: Jan.–Feb. 1988), 40.

2. Barbara Johnson, *Where Does a Mother Go to Resign?,* (Minneapolis, MN: Bethany House Publishers, 1979).

3. Recently I conducted a seminar at Church on the Rock in Lubbock, Texas. This church is associated with Larry Lea, author of the excellent book on prayer, *Could You Not Tarry One Hour?* (Altamont Springs, FL: Creation House, 1987). I would also like to recommend Evelyn Christiansen's book, *What Happens When Women Pray,* (Wheaton, IL: Victor Books, 1975). On this subject of prayer there are also several excellent books written by Dr. Paul Yonggi Cho.

CHAPTER FIVE

1. William Morrow, *Treasured Thoughts for Today, Tomorrow, and Always,* (Kansas City, MO: Hallmark Edition, 1974), 34.

2. Isaiah 64:6.

3. David Seamands, *Healing for Damaged Emotions,* (Wheaton, IL: Victor Books, 1981).

4. Dr. Maurice E. Wagner, *The Sensation of Being Somebody,* (Grand Rapids, MI: The Zondervan Corporation, 1975).

5. Dr. D. James Kennedy, Ph.D., pastoral message booklet "Self-Image (part one)", (Fort Lauderdale, FL: Coral Ridge Presbyterian Church).

CHAPTER SIX

1. Dr. Maurice E. Wagner, *The Sensation of Being Somebody,* (Grand Rapids, MI: The Zondervan Corporation, 1975), 13.

2. Dr. Robert Hemfelt, Dr. Frank Minirth, and Dr. Paul Meier, *Love Is a Choice,* (Nashville, TN: Thomas Nelson, Inc., 1989).

3. Hedy Nuriel, quoted in "The Modesto Bee" (March 9, 1989): Section A, 8.

4. Numbers 13:31,33.

CHAPTER SEVEN

1. Eleanor Roosevelt, *Treasured Thoughts for Today, Tomorrow, and Always,* (Kansas City, MO: Hallmark Editions, 1974), 36.

2. C. S. Lewis, *The Four Loves,* (London, England: Geoffrey Bles, 1960), 138–139.

3. Tom Wilson, Intimacy workshop material, (Salem, OR: First Church of the Nazarene, 1986).

4. "Modesto Bee" (April 11, 1990): Section B, 3.

CHAPTER EIGHT

1. Thomas Hughes, *Treasured Thoughts for Today, Tomorrow, and Always,* (Kansas City, MO: Hallmark Editions, 1974), 21.

2. "Lifewire" newsletter, Christian Singles Alive, (Salem, OR: First Church of the Nazarene, March 1988), 2.

3. Charles McCabe quoted In article by Juliet V. Allen, (Salem, OR. "Statesman-Journal," Nov. 1982).

4. Dinah Maria Mulock Craik, "Friendship," *Treasured Thoughts For Today, Tomorrow, and Always,* (Kansas City, MO: Hallmark Editions, 1974), 19.

CHAPTER NINE

1. Another keynote speaker at the European conference was Roger Crawford, who is the author of *Playing from the Heart,* (Prima Publishing Co., 1989). Roger was born

without hands and with deformed legs. He also had one leg amputated so that he could learn to walk. Against all odds, he became a tennis champion and the only severely handicapped athlete *ever* to reach professional certification as a pro from the U.S. Professional Tennis Association.

Also speaking at the conference were Clebe and Deanna McClary. Clebe was a Vietnam war hero who lost an arm and one eye on the battlefield. His wife, Deanna, and daughter, Tara, had just won the 1990 "Mother/Daughter U.S.A." pageant. Together they shared their stories about starting over. I would recommend that you read Deanna McClary's book, *Commitment to Love*, (Nashville, TN: Thomas Nelson, Inc., 1989).

2. *The Life & Times of Beethoven,* Portraits of Greatness, (Curtis Publishing Co., 1967), 44.

3. Tom Wilson, newspaper advertisement announcing First Church of the Nazarene worship services, (Salem, OR: "Statesman-Journal", 1987).

4. Marjorie P. K. Weiser and Jean S. Arbeiter, *Womanlist,* (Atheneum, 1981), 115.

APPENDIX

1. Reprinted with permission from The Single Life Institute. Copies of "Hate Divorce, But Love the Divorced" may be obtained by writing to TSLI, P.O. Box 2832, Abilene, TX, 79604.

ORDER TODAY!

For more information about having Joanne Wallace speak to your church or organization, please fill out the following order form.

☐ I'm interested in having Joanne Wallace come and speak in my area.

☐ I'm interested in cassette albums and other books by Joanne Wallace.

My name is: _____

My church or organization is: _____

_____

My address is: _____

City: _____ State: _____ Zip: _____

Home phone: ( )_____ Work Phone: ( )_____

MAIL TO:

Joanne Wallace
Speaker's Office
P.O. Box 2213
Fremont, CA 94536
(510) 551-0127

For information about becoming an Image Improvement consultant, or for the address of the Image consultant nearest you, send your name and address to:

Image Improvement, Inc.
P. O. Box 4536
Camp Hill, PA 17011
(717) 737-6764